Downsizing Mom:
A Tale of Clutter, Conflict, and Family Legacy

DANIELA FRITTER

A Russian Hill Press Book
United States • United Kingdom • Australia

 Russian Hill Press

Copyright © 2025 by Daniela Fritter

No part of this book maybe reproduced or stored in a retrieval system or transmitted in any form or by any means, electronic, mechanical photocopying, recording, or otherwise, without express written permission of the author.

The events, locations, and conversations in this book, while real, are recreated from the author's memory. The essence of the story, and the feelings and emotions evoked, are intended to be accurate representations. In certain instances, names, persons, organizations, and places have been changed to protect an individual's privacy. This work is free from AI-generated content.

ISBN: 979-8-9986955-0-6 (softcover)
ISBN: 979-8-9986955-1-3 (eBook)

Library of Congress Control Number: 2025908529

Cover Design: Tatiana Villa, Villa Design

DEDICATION

to those who have been profoundly befuddled by a parent

CONTENTS

Acknowledgments	1
Prologue	3
ONE	9
The Idea	
TWO	15
The Blinders Come Off	
THREE	23
Down the Rabbit Hole	
FOUR	29
The Papers	
FIVE	39
The Cancer	
SIX	49
The Books	
SEVEN	53
Preparing for Inspection	
EIGHT	61
The Accents on Words	
NINE	81
Memento	
TEN	91
The Tupperware	

ELEVEN	99
My Father	
TWELVE	109
The Pod	
THIRTEEN	113
Almost Showtime	
FOURTEEN	125
Making Room	
FIFTEEN	133
Mom's Retirement Speech	
SIXTEEN	141
The Proteins	
SEVENTEEN	147
Unhappiness	
EIGHTEEN	153
The Bangladesh Trip	
NINETEEN	161
A Week in Orange County	
TWENTY	167
Parenting 101	
TWENTY-ONE	181
My Grandmother	
TWENTY-TWO	195
Unmasking	

TWENTY-THREE	205
The Offer	
TWENTY-FOUR	211
Missing Pieces	
TWENTY-FIVE	219
Unlocking Doors	
TWENTY-SIX	227
Back in the Saddle	
TWENTY-SEVEN	237
The Signing	
TWENTY-EIGHT	245
The Strawberry-Washing Bowls	
TWENTY-NINE	253
Dad's Last Wishes	
THIRTY	259
Helping Hands	
THIRTY-ONE	265
The Final Days	
THIRTY-TWO	275
Just a Couple of Hours Cleaning	
THIRTY-THREE	285
Sunset	
Epilogue	295
Afterword	303
About the Author	305

ACKNOWLEDGMENTS

When I moved to Livermore in 2017, I started attending the monthly Whistlestop Writers Open Mic hosted by Cynthia Patton, Livermore's Poet Laureate at the time. After decades of writing technical and scientific documents for work, I was inspired by the supportive environment and the diversity of readings to try my hand at creative writing and poetry.

I signed up for writing classes taught by Barbara Flores through the city of Livermore. By the end of the final session, I realized it was impossible to adequately convey the character of my mother in a short story—I would need to write a full-length book.

Some of us from the class formed a small writing critique group. I'm grateful to Jean, the late Judy, and Rose (who joined the group through Judy) for their considerable help on my first draft. I shared a partial first draft with several other people who offered encouragement, particularly Jane and Carrie, whose enthusiastic support was not only validating but a source of motivation through the remaining years of writing and revising.

My developmental editor, Jordan Rosenfeld, made excellent suggestions that strengthened the story arc and improved the chapter transitions and overall flow. The STEM critique group of the California Writers Club Tri-Valley Branch provided invaluable feedback on my revisions and on additional chapters I decided to write, with special thanks to Ilana and Damon for their comprehensive review of the second draft. My copy editor, Patricia Boyle, did a wonderful job of cleaning up formatting, punctuation, and inconsistencies, and checked all my reference links. Paula Chinick of Russian Hill Press is responsible for the professional appearance of the finished product and walked me through the steps of publication.

I'm thankful to my family for their support, especially those I pestered for their memories and family knowledge (or to vet mine) in the pursuit of as much accuracy as possible: Mike, Andy, Leah, and Julie.

Finally, I'm indebted to my mother, who surprised me in all the ways described in this book.

PROLOGUE

Midway City, California, circa 1980. I'm home after school, babysitting my two younger brothers while Mom takes classes at the college. Today she comes home with a question for me.

"My psychology professor said we should ask other people what they think of us."

I blink in surprise. We don't ever talk about that kind of stuff.

"So, Daniela," she says, "what do you think about me?"

I stare at her blankly as my mind skitters around for something to say. The leaf-raking incident from a few weeks ago pops into my head.

I was in my room doing algebra homework. I heard a knock on my door and Mom came in. She looked flustered.

"How am I supposed to get to the washing machine? There are leaves all over the backyard."

My heart skipped a beat. *Did I tell her I'd rake them? I don't remember that.* I looked out the window toward our detached garage where the washing machine was, about fifty feet from the house. The path was covered with leaves. I turned to face her, keeping my expression blank and my voice steady. "Did you want me to rake them?"

"If it's not too much *trouble*," she said with a sarcastic head wobble. "I know you're so very *busy*."

She closed the door with a thud.

Geez. Can't she just ask straightforwardly? Why does she always act like I did something wrong?

I looked down at the sheet of paper on my desk. Numbers, letters, and symbols, arranged in a specific order and manipulated according to rules and logic. Math was straightforward—you set up the problem and worked through the steps until you got the answer. It made sense. Not like people. I stared at the half-finished problem to see if I could figure out the next step, but I couldn't concentrate. Mom would be back any minute to see why I was still in my room.

I got the rake from the garage and started pulling the tines across the leaves. *It's not a big deal. All parents boss their kids around. It's not like she yelled at me or called me names. I have no reason to feel bad. No reason at all.*

I made a mound of leaves next to the garage and moved on to the next section. But darn it, it made me mad, the way she talked to me. Like I was supposed to just *know* she wanted the leaves raked, and to do it before she even asked. *Outrageous!*

Or did she tell me to do it earlier, and I forgot? Now I was doubting myself. I frowned. *She's messing with my head again.*

I moved on to the next section of lawn, fuming. Mom would be in a happy mood when I went back inside. She had needed something done and I was doing it; now everything was right with the world. It sure didn't feel that way to me. But complaining always made things worse.

I sighed. Nothing to be done about it.

Mom is looking at me, waiting to hear what I think of her. I can't possibly say, "domineering and dismissive." I know what she wants to hear, because she declares it often enough: that she's a warm and nurturing mother who's done everything out of love for her children. This, I also can't say—it sounds bizarre and unreal.

In desperation, my gaze falls on the piles of books and papers on top of and under side tables, the boxes stacked in corners and behind chairs, and the knickknacks on every surface.

"You're a pack rat," I blurt out, and my heart sinks. I've blown my chance to say something meaningful and let her know how I feel. But I have no clue how to say such things.

"Oh," she says, visibly disappointed. "Anything else?"

"Nothing I can think of."

She turns to go. "You're right. I do have a lot of stuff."

PART I

Thirteen Weekends of Decluttering

ONE

The Idea

October - December 2018

I'm in line at the fancy deli in Big Sur, waiting to order coffee and a breakfast pastry before the three-hour drive home to Livermore. I'm not fully present. My mind drifts through the events of yesterday: celebratory shots of Scotch with the family to mark the end of my son's bachelorhood, the wedding ceremony officiated by the couple's siblings under two towering redwood trees, the outdoor reception with the artichoke-themed food truck, and dancing into the night. I had my concerns about having a wedding out here, in this mountainy rustic town off a winding coastal highway so far from everything, but it worked out beautifully.

No thanks to me. The siblings organized the ceremony, and the bride's family did the rest of the event planning. I was grateful, since I was still recovering from the craziness of last year: remodeling, selling, buying, moving, divorce. What a relief to be done with 2017. Now I'm single with my own little house and a good job. The kids are grown and on their own, and I have no one to look after but myself. The thought makes me smile.

Someone walks into my bubble and breaks my reverie. It's my brother Andy, holding his sleepy five-year-old son against his chest. He has something on his mind.

"What would you think about Mom selling her house and moving to Southern California into a retirement community near me?"

"Hmm," I nod, trying to process the idea.

"Mom's getting older. That house is too much for her to take care of anymore."

True, now that I think about it. Mom is almost eighty-three, with recent eye and back problems that make her day-to-day life more difficult.

"What worries me is her driving," I tell him. "She still takes her car out every day to do her shopping and activities. San Jose is too big and too busy for her to be out in that traffic. Just turning left out of her cul-de-sac is a hazard—the house on the corner has a new fence that blocks the view of oncoming cars."

"So, you agree? I think it'll be the best thing for her. If she moves out and leaves all that excess stuff behind, it'll be a huge burden off her shoulders. She'll move into a senior community with only the things she needs and be free to make new friends and enjoy her life. I'll get her and the kids together every couple of weeks so they can get to know each other and have a closer relationship."

I feel a twinge of guilt about not seeing Mom more often. I make the forty-five-minute drive to her house maybe once a month, which seems to be our plateau. We've made our peace, though, and I'm okay with her moving away to someplace where she'll get more attention.

I tell Andy I have no objections, and he goes to pitch the idea to Mom who is waiting for me at one of the wooden tables outside. I wonder if anything will come of it.

Mom doesn't take to the idea of moving right away. After her divorce from Dad in the late '70s, she went back to school part-time and eventually earned her law degree. She bought the small two-bedroom house in San Jose in 1992 as a recently minted attorney and empty-nester. By the time she retired, she had a big enough nest egg to continue the monthly mortgage payments until the house was paid off. She had friends in the area and was involved in church, music groups, and community activities. There was no reason to move.

Now, after twenty-six years in the house, she's slowed down, and most of her friends and the longtime neighbors she was close to have moved or died. In the weeks following Andy's suggestion, she talks about the possibility of moving at every opportunity, turning it over and over in her mind and making it more comfortable.

"Do you think I should sell the house and move

to Southern California?" she asks during my next visit.

"There are good reasons to do so." I reiterate them, with Andy's kids at the top of the list. Then we talk about reasons to stay, of which there are fewer.

"What about you?" she says. "Will you be lonely?"

"Don't worry about me. My kids live nearby. And you and I can still talk on the phone."

"So I should go."

"It's really up to you."

"Okay," she says. I can't tell if that means she's decided or she's still thinking about it, but I don't ask. I don't want to seem eager to have her move away.

In early December she tells me, "I think I should do it."

She invites me over to help her go through her clothes. Mom hasn't asked me for organizing help since the linen closet episode ten years ago. That had been two hours of torture. I remember standing there, bored and irritated, as she chattered away about where she'd gotten one or the other set of sheets, why certain of them were mismatched, that she wanted to keep ones of the wrong size because they were pretty and she might have a bed that size one day, and asking me what she should do with heirloom embroidered cloth napkins and tablecloths from our family that were old and stained and didn't fit with anything in the house. I didn't care about any of that. I made half-hearted recommendations which she dismissed half the time. Why was I even there? It was a colossal waste of my time. But she was energized by my presence and pleased with the results. She offered to come to my house and help me organize *my* linens. I didn't take her up on it, and she didn't ask me for help organizing anything again. Until now.

We spend three hours in the master bedroom while she tries on various pieces to get my advice on fit and style, which she ignores if she doesn't agree. Once again she elaborates on the history of certain items: the dark blue sequined dress and matching jacket she wore once to a fancy banquet, her mother's clothes that she kept after her death but that don't quite fit and aren't her style, the hand-knitted scarf that was a present from a neighbor, the purple velour pantsuit passed on from a friend who didn't want it anymore. But this time I'm not bothered. I even find some of her tidbits interesting. How weird that my experience is influenced so strongly by my feelings for Mom. Ten years ago, when hostilities simmered just below the surface, her sorting process drove me insane. Now I feel calm and patient, with a sense of satisfaction that I'm doing something to help her.

I keep track of the stacks of clothes on her bed and make periodic trips to my car with the discards. When we're done, I drive away with a carload for donation, mostly her old business suits, clothes from a heavier phase, and outfits from the '80s and '90s with baggy pants and shoulder pads. She still has too many clothes—does one really need six white dress blouses in retirement?—but it's a good start. Or so I think.

TWO

The Blinders Come Off

December 2018

A couple of weeks later, I'm headed back to Mom's to pick up my brother Mike. He's been at her house for a couple of days after flying in from the East Coast for the holidays, and he'll spend the next four or five days at my house. I didn't want Mom to feel like I was in a hurry to leave, so I suggested we have lunch together before Mike and I go.

Mike answers the door and gives me a weary smile. I step in for a hug and notice how stiff he is. I try to glimpse his face, but he's already turned away.

Inside, I find Mom in the kitchen holding a dish towel and looking lost.

"Hi, Mom."

She looks at me. "I'm running behind. I can't get in the laundry room. The Swiffer fell across the door, and I've been trying to get in there for an hour."

It's not unusual for Mom to be behind schedule, or to be so distracted she forgets to greet me. But it's odd she hasn't asked Mike for help. He frowns and goes to have a look. The door opens inward a few inches, then is blocked by a horizontal rod wedged between the wall and the washing machine. Mike reaches through the narrow opening and fiddles with the rod. In less than a minute, the door is open.

"Oh, *thank* you," Mom says to him, hand on her heart. "What would I do without you?"

"Mm hmm."

Mom takes care of her laundry task, then turns her attention to lunch. "Do you like this quinoa and brown rice mix from Costco?" she asks, showing us the package. "Do you think it will go with the salmon burgers? If not, I have frozen salmon steaks, but they'll take an extra thirty minutes to defrost." She retrieves separate packages of green beans and cauliflower from the fridge. "The cauliflower is older, but do you think there'll be enough for everyone after trimming?" She rummages around in the pantry. "I have a carton of this Latin-style black bean soup from Trader Joe's. We can warm it up and eat it as a soup or just pour it over the food as a sauce. What do you think of that?"

By the time she asks what fruit we want for dessert, we say yes to the first one she picks up. Or at least I do—Mike has stopped responding. She looks over at him.

"Mike?" she says. "What about you?"

"It's fine," he says, frowning.

She's still holding the pear. "Or you could have an apple. Would that be better?"

"It's *fine*," he repeats.

"What about grapefruit?"

"It's. *Fine*."

She pauses, then says, "I'm sorry I don't have any fruit you like."

"All this fussing about food again," he says. "I don't need fruit after a full meal. It's *fine*."

I feel nauseous. Mike's been putting up with this for two days, and I prolonged it by suggesting lunch with Mom. I'll have to apologize to him later.

"The pear is good," I say to Mom in my most neutral voice. I take a few steps toward the fridge to signal that we should start preparing the food, and Mike excuses himself to pack his things. Mom and I confer about meal logistics: where to make space on the kitchen counter, whether to pan fry or bake the salmon burgers, which knife, bowl, or pan to use, how small to cut the green beans, and a reminder of how to use the microwave vegetable steamer. I handle the food-related tasks while Mom focuses on where to move the clutter on the dining table and chairs, which plates and cutlery to use, what drinks to offer.

Half an hour later, everything is ready. The three of us sit down at the table and Mom says a short blessing. We eat in silence for a while, then Mom turns to me with an expectant smile.

"When do you think you can come over after the holidays? I have more clothes to go through." She pauses, then adds, "Don't you think I've made good progress?"

Mike doesn't give me a chance to answer. He raises his eyebrows at her and says, "Maybe you've made some progress with the clothes, but you haven't even made a dent in the stuff you have in this house. If you're serious about downsizing, you need to radically pick up the pace of getting rid of things."

Mom nods for emphasis as she replies. "I know what you're saying, and I agree with you a hundred percent. But I'm not young anymore. I can't get around as easily as I used to. I never thought I'd have a bad back."

"The physical problems are only part of it," Mike counters. "You need to change your attitude about your possessions. Think more in terms of throwing things away rather than reorganizing them. Otherwise, you'll just end up rearranging everything and never get it done."

They go on for a few minutes, rehashing their points and talking past each other. I try to be inconspicuous—the argument is futile, and I don't want to be dragged in. I'll talk to Mike about it on the way home.

At the end of the meal, Mom and I split the pear; it's ripe to perfection and delicious, even though I'm full. Mom doesn't want help with the dishes, so we say our goodbyes.

Once we're in my car and out of sight, Mike and I breathe a mutual sigh of relief. I'd gathered from his coolness toward Mom that they had an altercation before I got there, and I wait for him to speak.

"Man, we got into it the first night," he says. "As

soon as I arrived, before I even said or did anything, she started in with, 'Why are you here, I know you don't want to be here, you just can't wait to leave, why don't you just take my car and bring it back before you fly home?'"

"Oh, no."

"You know, though," he continues, "Mom makes a lot of wrong assumptions, but sometimes she picks up on something real. I *was* dreading going to her house. I felt it on the plane."

"I know what you mean," I nod. "There's a part of me that's still on edge when I go visit."

"It's exhausting dealing with her emotional issues."

"For sure. The clutter, too, maybe?"

Mike groans. "She has so much stuff. It's like I can't move without worrying about knocking something over. She's got stacks of papers everywhere. There are boxes of stuff on the floor, clothes and things hanging from the doorknobs, and washed-out plastic containers in stacks on the kitchen counter. All the surfaces are covered with stuff, and you can't find what you really need. I can't find the soap in the bathroom!"

Mike's vehemence gives me pause. I mentally review the scene inside the house. Stacks of mail and papers everywhere—on the kitchen table, on the makeshift brick-and-board shelf next to the table, on the shelving unit next to the love seat, and on the shelf under the microwave. Older stacks in the living room alternate with towers of books to create a landscape of high-rises. They cover a piano that's never been played and a couch that hasn't been sat on in fifteen years. The remaining horizontal surfaces are sprinkled with never-lit candles, small figurines, empty vases, gift boxes of chocolate, orchids, handbags, and eyeglasses cases. Sweaters and shirts hang on hangers from doorknobs. On the floor are boxes of all shapes and sizes, strategically stacked to leave the most space for walking; they contain papers, old magazines, and knickknacks. Inside the fridge are shelves filled high and deep with containers of measured-out food portions and leftovers, rewashed Ziploc bags holding rinsed perishables wrapped in paper towels, and a small open bucket of food waste hidden from the ants until trash day.

Mike was right—it had gotten significantly worse than it was in our childhood. Like the frog in slowly heating water, I'd become acclimated to it. I could no longer find a place on Mom's kitchen counter to put an extra bowl or serving plate while I prepared us a meal, or a surface on which to put a piece of paper where it wouldn't sink into the background and get lost. But the only sign that this was making me anxious was my deep breathing after leaving her house to loosen my constricted chest muscles.

"You're right," I say to Mike. "The clutter is bad. But let me see if I can work with her and move things along."

"I spent whole days of my Christmas vacation one year helping her clear some shelves in the garage," he grouses, "and the next year they were full of crap again."

"Ugh."

He sighs, then chops the air with his hand as he speaks. "She managed to raise three kids while going to school and getting a law degree, then held down a full-time job for thirteen years. She should be capable of dealing with her own stuff."

"You would think." I pause. "Maybe the idea of moving will motivate her. If she wants it badly enough, she'll get down to business."

He shakes his head. "Even if by some miracle that happened, it won't accomplish anything in the long run. Give her a couple of months in the new place and the clutter will be back."

I say nothing. I can't even think that far ahead.

THREE

Down the Rabbit Hole

January - April 2019

In January, I take the baby step of offering to go to Mom's for an afternoon every other weekend to help her downsize, in hopes this will spur some planning and organizing on her part. Instead, she greets me with lists of things to help her with that have little to do with downsizing. Such as exchanging the hall lightbulb for a brighter one. Or organizing her tax receipts. And a recurring favorite from the past: helping her navigate computer accounts and new technology she can't resist acquiring while I stick to my old technology that works because I find it draining to keep learning and troubleshooting new systems. Thanks to Mom and YouTube, I now know how to resync a Roku remote by removing and reinserting the batteries and turning things on and off in a particular order.

Our pattern over the next few months is

unchanging. I race through her to-do lists, then ask what downsizing tasks we should tackle. She gives me a blank look and says she doesn't know. I putz around, trying to find things to do in a universe of things that need doing. She rejects all my suggestions as tasks we should do later, or that she wants to do herself and then doesn't. She gets my hopes up once when she asks me to move a heavy chair so she can access the stacks of papers and magazines behind it after I leave, but they are in the same state next time I show up.

"Don't you think we've made good progress?" she starts saying sometime in the spring. I scrunch my face and make non-committal sounds. I know her cheery refrain is more about having worked on something together than achieving actual goals, but I don't want her to mislead anybody about how much we're getting done. Which isn't much at all.

One weekend I take a pen and notepad, and we go through the house together, taking stock of what needs to be done. My list is crude—each room has four to eight bullet points that designate broad categories of items to be sorted, donated, packed, or needing a decision—but it's something objective I can point to when Mom puts me on the spot about our progress. She eventually modifies her stock phrase to: "Don't you think we've made good progress, considering?" Somehow I find this less aggravating and easier to agree with.

At the end of April, after months of receiving my lukewarm emails about our progress, Andy sends us an email introduction to Cindy, a real estate agent he's worked with in the Bay Area. "I've told her about the situation. She's very knowledgeable about the market and can give you an idea of what kind of renovations the house needs and the best time to sell it. She's available to meet you and see the house this Saturday at 10 a.m. Can you confirm that this time would work for you both?"

On the drive to Mom's on Saturday morning, I try to decipher what I'm feeling. My first thought: leave it to Andy to force the issue. My second thought: I can't really blame him—Mom and I don't have much to show for the last five months. Besides, Andy did offer to help, and I rebuffed him.

"Give me one weekend," he'd said. "I'll come up and rent a dumpster. It'd be ideal if you could convince Mom to leave the house."

"No way," I told him. "She's not going to agree to that." His suggestion made me feel strangely protective of her.

So instead, he found us a realtor. Which is not a bad idea. Andy can do the vetting and oversee the formal parts of the real estate process, which leaves Mom and me less to deal with.

As I pull up to Mom's house, I imagine seeing everything through the realtor's eyes. The house is at the end of a cul-de-sac in a modest suburban neighborhood. The outside is reasonably well maintained and doesn't stand out in any way. But when I walk through the front door, all I see is the clutter.

Cindy arrives soon after, with her mane of frizzy red hair and chunky black boots. Her face doesn't show any reaction to the mess. She steps deftly around the things on the floor to survey the rooms. "The beginning of August would be the best time to put the house on the market," she tells us. "You'll need to get ninety percent of the stuff out."

Neither of these statements come as a surprise, but I hadn't put them together in my head before. Now I see the writing on the wall. If we plod along the way we have been, downsizing will take years. Mom will miss her window of opportunity to bond with Andy's kids while they're young. She'll eventually need help with meals and cleaning and driving. Better if she's in a senior living residence where those are already in place, rather than having to coordinate in-home services piecemeal in a house that will also require maintenance. Cindy's suggested target date gives us the prodding we need to get serious and make it happen. I'll have to take charge. I'll also need to give up my weekends for the foreseeable future, but somehow I'm okay with that. I've come to realize I have another motivation for diving into this downsizing project.

My relationship with Mom is much better than it used to be. But I don't understand why we had the problems we did. And we don't see each other often enough for me to figure it out. Going through Mom's things together will be an opportunity to revisit the past, to help me figure out what makes her tick and react the way she does, and just maybe to solve this puzzle of our relationship.

For the next three months, I leave my house Saturday mornings about 9 or 10 and come back

Sunday evenings at 8 or 9. If it's been a productive weekend, my car is full of things to recycle, donate, or trash. Since my waste gets picked up on Mondays, I grab a glass of wine after I get home and go back outside to spend fifteen or twenty minutes stuffing mountains of papers, bundled plastic bags, stacks of plastic containers, dusty disintegrating cardboard boxes, and pieces of random wood into my recycle bin to haul to the curb.

The remaining stuff gets driven around in my car for the rest of the week because I'm too tired to deal with it. It's mostly donations for Goodwill but still requires sorting before I drop it off. At the beginning, I get it done by Friday night. Over time, piles form and grow in my house for me to attend to when I have more energy.

Some things are not good enough for Goodwill—they are old and icky and falling apart. Yet Mom insists, "Oh, someone could use that," or "That can be washed," referring to the deflated mini-soccer ball with the polygonal panels peeling off, or "They can fix that," to the pile of yellow plastic beads that was once a costume jewelry necklace. I'll agree with her but only to get them out of her house so they can go into my trash.

Some items are considered hazardous waste and need special handling: heaps of old electronics, cleaning products leaking out of cracked plastic bottles with faded labels, and crusty batteries.

Then there are the things I decide to keep: aromatherapy oils I can massage onto my pulse points to become relaxed, energized, sensual, or enlightened; a piece of knitting, yellow with multicolored flecks, that forms the front half of an infant onesie meant for me and never finished; a guidebook for avoiding unflattering clothing styles for each body type; plastic covers to keep dust off the shoulders of rarely worn clothes; classics I should read one day, like *Frankenstein* and *The Feminine Mystique*.

There's a villain hand puppet from my childhood with a pointy hat, an even pointier nose, and a sneer showing teeth on one side of his soft plastic head. "Donate it," I had told Mom many times. "I don't want it, and my kids won't want it." Yet now I have it, and I want to keep it. Not because it reminds me of my childhood, but because it symbolizes something I want to learn to appreciate: Mom's efforts to be a good mother.

As we go through Mom's stuff, sorting and packing and rearranging each weekend, we spend more quality time together than at any time since I moved out at age twenty. Over three decades later, I'm getting to know her all over again. And seeing old things, like our relationship, in a new light.

FOUR

The Papers

May 2019

Mom has been burdened by her papers for years. I started hearing about them in the early '00s, not long after she retired. She would share her plans for the week, then say, "And, I need to work on the papers." I never asked what she meant; it seemed obvious from the stacks I saw in her kitchen and living room.

When we take inventory at the start of downsizing, I count forty boxes of papers inside the house, plus another forty in the garage. The additional paper stacks visible throughout the house and hidden behind cabinet doors would bring it to a hundred boxes, easily. This makes me anxious, so when I have a moment, I distract myself with a calculation. One hundred boxes of printer paper equals five-hundred-thousand sheets of paper, enough to cover 6.8 football fields in a single layer. Oof.

Mom surveys the boxes we've pulled into the open and shakes her head. "I don't even want to tell you what I think about myself." She chuckles, then reprimands herself: "How could you *do* this?"

Yes indeed, I think, *how could you?* But I say nothing. She's sensitive about it, and we have a long way to go. I remind myself about the boxes in my own garage that need going through and give her what I hope is an empathetic smile. It's just a matter of degree, isn't it?

A few weekends later we discover a second layer of boxes in the back of the closet in the master bedroom. We open them and look inside.

"Oh, no," she groans. "More papers. I can't believe it. This is just awful." She gives me a bashful look as I stifle my irritation. "I promise I'll never do this again."

That makes me smile. "What a relief."

Mom refuses at first to let me go through the boxes; she wants to do it herself since there are personal things inside. But after weeks of working on other stuff and seeing the papers shrink by only a couple of stacks in the living room, I finagle a way in. Some of the older boxes have deformed or split open, so in the guise of moving the contents to new boxes, I start sorting.

"You don't really need these *US and World News* magazines or mail order catalogs from the '90s, do you?" After a moment, she says no, and I realize I've been holding my breath. "How about these old bills and statements?"

She gives me her blessing to dispose of them if they are more than seven years old, although if they show her full social security or credit card number as was routine not so long ago, they go into a Red Dog box for shredding instead of the recycle bin. Those that are less than seven years old go back into their envelopes and into one of seven shoe boxes in the corner of the living room marked by the year from 2012 to 2018. "I have a system now," she tells me.

I continue through the first box, making increasingly more decisions while she occupies herself with other things. The papers are loose and unsorted, preserved chronologically the way they were encountered in time. I might have guessed this from the way some boxes are labelled by location and year, as in *Bedroom table 1986*. I look at every single item and open every ambiguous envelope to make sure I don't throw out anything important.

It takes me nearly three hours to get to the bottom of the box. Is this reasonable? I do another calculation. Three hours for one box of printer paper works out to two seconds per sheet. I mentally construct a mathematical model using matrix algebra and categorize the contents by evaluation time. Magazines and PennySaver coupon books are less than one second per page, since there are multiple pages. Advertising circulars, shopping lists, and church bulletins are one second each. Programs from concerts in which she sang in the choir and other mementos related to her activities in various clubs and organizations count as two seconds. Bills and statements require a decision tree and average closer to four seconds. Given these parameters, two to three hours per box seems about right.

I lament to Andy over the phone and tell him how many boxes there are, preparing him for the likelihood that Mom will take some of them with her when she moves.

"You should just dump them," he tells me. "If she hasn't gone into a box in ten or twenty years, it probably doesn't have anything in it that she needs."

"But the papers aren't organized. Everything is mixed together—important things in between junk mail and old newspapers. Personal letters, pictures, and memorabilia, the kinds of things someone of Mom's age would want to take out and reminisce over."

Andy, who has his own personal limit of one box of keepsakes, is not sold. "Mom wouldn't remember most of this stuff if it disappeared. It would be such a relief for her not to have to deal with it anymore."

I try again, lest he resurrect the dumpster idea. "Mom says her naturalization certificate is in one of those boxes. And also the home improvement receipts to offset the capital gains after she sells the house."

"She can get a replacement copy of the naturalization certificate. And the IRS should accept estimates for the home improvement work."

"Okay, then, what about the old work stubs and retirement statements with her full social security number on them? We can't just shred entire boxes—there's a hundred of them. Do you know how expensive that would be?"

He doesn't have a response for that.

I continue to go through the boxes, a few at a time, fitting them in between other things we're doing. In the weeks to come, we find Mom's naturalization certificate and her living trust documents, almost all her home improvement receipts, compiled from many boxes and totaling over $50,000, and old family pictures and historical documents, including official citizenship papers and rationing tickets from World War II for food and clothes.

I come across newspaper clippings on topics she found of interest; starting in the '90s these were joined by printouts of online articles. One in particular catches my eye: a book review of *Dirty Secret: A Daughter Comes Clean about Her Mother's Compulsive Hoarding*. I am tempted to bring this up with her but decide against it. Maybe I'll buy the book.

Here and there I unearth a cache of documents that takes me back to the past. In one box I find monthly newsletters, activity information packets, event flyers, and meeting notes from Parents Without Partners, a support group for single parents that Mom was involved with. She would take us to their family socials and leave us to our own devices as she made the rounds. One potluck stands out in my memory.

Middle-aged men and women gathered in clusters around picnic tables at the park, eating and talking. Kids ran around playing, my brothers among them—one on the monkey bars, the other throwing Frisbees. The few teenagers kept to themselves, giving off leave-me-alone vibes.

I found a quiet spot to sit under a tree near one of the picnic tables. I plucked a blade of grass and examined the fibers running along it. Then I plucked another. And another. Then I heard Mom's voice. She'd drifted over to my picnic table and was talking about me to another mom.

"Daniela is such a wonderful daughter!" she exclaimed, glancing my way with an adoring smile.

I pretended I didn't hear and busied myself weaving the grass strips into a braid. I couldn't let myself bask in her praise. She was a fraud. She was acting like yesterday never happened. Yesterday when she called me a horrible and hateful daughter. For no reason, really. What it usually came down to was that I wasn't catering to her enough.

"She's such a help at home," Mom continued. "She babysits her brothers so I can go to my college classes."

Harumph. I wasn't falling for her sweet talk—she was not forgiven. I got up and made my way to the pine trees on the other side of the park. I sat and weaved tiny mats out of pine needles until I was bored.

Back at the picnic tables I surveyed the dessert offerings when someone sidled up to me. It was the woman Mom had been talking to earlier. "You are so lucky to have such a sweet mom!" said she who had known her all of ten minutes.

I didn't know what to say, and I was afraid of what she'd see if I looked her in the eye. I studied the bark on the ground and let my hair hang in my face until she went away.

Mom sure knew how to charm people. It drove me crazy nobody understood what went on in private. How was I supposed to explain it to them? And for what purpose? It wasn't like anyone was going to come and rescue me. I was on my own.

Mom's habit of printing out her email conversations provides occasional nuggets as I go through the boxes. Some of the exchanges are innocuous, like making plans with coworkers. Others are contentious, including email spats she had with me that I recognize and tuck discreetly into my overnight bag to review when I get back home.

On May 7, 2011, Mom wrote to me in an email: "I received your card for Mother's Day. I opened it today. I wish I had not done that. Can you please elaborate: What do you think is the Mother's Day I deserve?"

I cringed when I read her words, imagining her looking at me with wounded, accusing eyes. I had stood in the card aisle of the drug store, picking up one after another with loving and flowery sentiments: "Celebrating the wonderful mother you are," "I'm so lucky to have you in my life," "I couldn't ask for a better mom," and "Thank you for being there every day with just the love I needed." I didn't feel any of these things. The thought of having to sign my name to one of them made me physically ill. Then I found a plain-spoken card that wouldn't make me lie, that I could send off to her in good conscience. It had the phrase, "Wishing you the Mother's Day you deserve," with flowers and nature scenery in pastel shades to convey that I wished her relaxation and enjoyment.

Her email continued: "I loved you before you were born, and every single day thereafter. To this day, I don't remember that you ever expressed any loving feeling toward me. Is that what you think I deserve? I hope your children treat you better than that." She signed off with, "Running out of love. Still your mother. Unfortunately for you, there is no way for me to undo that. P.S.: Fortunately for me, I have an appointment with my therapist next week. So don't you worry about me. Mother."

My heart pounded and my thoughts raced—so much for going to sleep at a reasonable hour. I composed my reply and sent it off at almost midnight: "I'm sorry you didn't like the card. You seem to appreciate cards for special occasions, so I thought sending you one would make you feel valued. I chose a simpler card since I'm not an overly flowery person. I think it's more meaningful to give time and attention than to use flowery words that anyone can say. But it looks like you equate love with overt expressions of affection, and if that's not there, you feel I'm mistreating you. Do you really think I mistreat you? Is there anything I do that you consider to be loving behavior? I'm sorry it's not enough."

In her email reply the next morning, she did a one-eighty: "You made my day by letting me know that the purpose of your card was to make me feel valued. Indeed, that is all I need to know, and it's very important to me." After saying she'd like to talk more about some of the things I said, but at my convenience, she told me to go ahead and enjoy my day, exclamation point.

With that, the skirmish was over, the transfer of bad feelings from her to me complete, once again. I obsessed about it for days afterwards—knowing I had screwed up with the choice of card, furious at her assumption that I meant it in a negative way, and scoffing at the ridiculous idea that anyone would send it with such intent. I struggled to figure out if I had a right to be hurt by the things she said or if I really was a crappy daughter. How was I almost fifty and had not figured out how to stay in her good graces? And then I kicked myself for letting it get to me.

I did not trust her invitation to talk more. What would be the point? I reread her email ad nauseam, anticipating all her arguments: "I've given you nothing but love, but all you give me back is your silence." "I'm just expressing my feelings. Are you trying to say I'm not allowed to speak up?" "I'm trying to get information because you don't tell me anything. Why would you feel hurt by that?" Or, her favorite trope of last resort, "Maybe I'm just too stupid to understand what's going on."

I turned my attention back to my life while I waited for the storm clouds in my head to dissipate, and that was that.

DOWNSIZING MOM

I stash Mom's email printout away in my desk at home, feeling a bit rattled. It's hard to believe we were engaged in this kind of strife as recently as eight years ago. And still might be if it weren't for the cancer.

FIVE

The Cancer

2013

In the spring of 2013, Mom asked me to accompany her to one of her doctor's appointments.

"I have this thing on my neck," she said, gingerly touching a plum-sized lump covering the hollow of her throat. "And it hurts. The doctor took a biopsy last week. If you can come with me to the appointment to hear the results, I won't have to worry about missing something."

I told her yes. Mom was self-reliant when it came to health matters, so the fact that she wanted me there was unusual. Six years earlier, when she was diagnosed with breast cancer and had a lumpectomy followed by a mastectomy, she kept me in the loop about what was going on, but she never asked for my help. I was surprised when Andy came up from Southern California to stay with her for a few days after the mastectomy. Had she asked him and not me? Or had he insisted on coming?

"When I heard about the surgery, I had to come," he told me. "This is a big deal."

Should *I* have insisted on helping? But she never held it against me that I didn't; if she had, I surely would have heard about it in the six years since. Nevertheless, I was ready to redeem myself.

At the appointment, the endocrinologist pulled up the pathology report on the computer. "The cells from your biopsy are consistent with papillary thyroid cancer, which would be a treatable cancer with a good prognosis. However, I'm very concerned with how quickly the tumor is growing. I suspect you might have a more aggressive variant."

He looked at us intently. I nodded for him to continue.

"I recommend scheduling a thyroidectomy as soon as possible. This would be a complete removal of the thyroid. You'll have to take a pill every day for the rest of your life to replace the thyroid hormone your body won't be making anymore."

I looked at Mom. She was gazing at him, calm and serene. It didn't seem like she had anything to say, so I nodded at him again. He spent the remainder of the appointment laying out the next steps. Once the surgery was scheduled, a pre-op appointment would be set up for the surgeon to tell us about the procedure and answer any questions we had. Post-op, Mom would be assigned an oncologist to oversee and coordinate her treatment with other specialists, and we'd go from there.

On leaving the doctor's office, I felt Mom was in

good hands. There was a plan, and the health professionals were going to guide us through it. After all, they got Mom through her breast cancer and there hadn't been a recurrence. Everything would be fine.

Once we were back at Mom's, she became animated. "Why does he want to take all of it out? If there's still healthy tissue, they'll be removing something I still need, and making me take thyroid hormone for the rest of my life when it's not necessary. Can't they just remove the bad part and leave the rest?"

I was immediately annoyed that Mom hadn't asked the doctor when she had the chance. Then I felt useless. I hadn't asked enough questions myself to know how to answer her. "Why don't we ask the surgeon at the pre-op appointment?"

At the appointment a couple of weeks later, the surgeon responded emphatically to Mom's question. "No. Both sides of your thyroid are grossly enlarged. The likelihood of finding something to salvage is next to nothing."

That was definitive enough for Mom.

I drove her to Kaiser early on the day of the surgery. After she went in to get prepped, I gave the medical assistant my cell phone number and went to the cafeteria to read a book. A few hours later I got a call that there had been a complication and Mom was still in surgery, but things were going well. A few hours after that, in mid-afternoon, I was informed she was coming out of the anesthesia, and I could visit her in the recovery room.

She was lying on the semi-reclined hospital bed,

propped up with pillows, with a big bandage on her neck. She looked at me as I walked up but otherwise didn't react. I hadn't expected her to speak, though I thought there'd be some sign—a smile, gesture, or expression in her eyes—that she recognized me. I sat in the chair by her bed as the nurses flitted about and occasionally came over to take her vitals and fluff her pillows. They talked in loud and cheery voices as if this were normal everyday stuff, but Mom's grogginess had me spooked.

They brought her beef broth for dinner. She took a few sips, then whispered, "It's too sweet. Did they put sugar in it?"

Okay, I thought. *Mom is still in there.*

When I came back the next day, she was more alert, although still not very talkative. In the afternoon, the surgeon came by.

"You were very lucky," she told Mom. "If we had known what we'd find when we opened you up, you would have been referred to palliative care instead of surgery."

I gaped at her. Palliative care meant managing a person's symptoms to make them more comfortable because they were out of treatment options. I looked at Mom. Her eyes were wide, but she said nothing.

The surgeon continued. "The tumor you had was not papillary cancer. It was one of the bad ones. We'll find out more from the pathology report in a few days. Normally we wouldn't attempt to remove such a tumor because it's already spread into the surrounding tissues. But since we had you open, I removed what I could and found it hadn't spread too far. I was able to leave most of your lymph nodes and other nearby structures intact." There would be more follow-ups with the oncologist and other specialists, but as for the surgeon, I felt impressed and indebted. Mom was lucky, indeed.

I spent the next few days at Mom's while she recuperated. I boiled and mashed and minced food for her to eat. I went outside with her for short walks. I laid in bed listening nervously through the wall for irregularities in her breathing and held my own breath when she had the occasional coughing fit.

The pathology report showed stage 4 anaplastic thyroid cancer, a rare and highly aggressive form with low survival rates and not much data on effective treatments. The oncologist forwarded us a few journal articles. I read through them carefully, frustrated that the case numbers were too low to get decent statistics. Most patients succumbed within three years. A small proportion (somewhere between 2 and 15 percent, possibly) were still alive seven years later, but the authors were not able to correlate that with any particular treatment. How was I supposed to advise Mom with that dearth of information? But it wasn't all on me.

The oncologist recommended a combined course of chemo and radiation to destroy residual cancer cells. "An aggressive therapy to combat an aggressive cancer," he said to Mom. "You'll likely only get one shot."

"I don't want chemo," Mom said firmly. "I've seen other people go through that. I don't want to die, of course. But if my time is up, so be it."

The oncologist consulted with the radiation specialist and came back with a proposal: no chemo, but double up on the radiation treatments. Mom agreed.

At Kaiser's Cancer Treatment Center, they made her a custom-fitted mask to immobilize her head so the x-rays would hit their target. She made the half-hour drive to get irradiated, twice a day, five days a week, for the next month. At home she kept to a rigorous protocol of pills, vitamins, glucosamine drinks, skin and dental care, voice and swallowing exercises, and a restrictive diet of soft foods low in iodine, supplemented by protein shakes. I went with her to all the appointments with the specialists and took meticulous notes that we reviewed at home, but I did little else to help with her day-to-day care as she wanted to manage it herself. By the end of the radiation treatments, she had lost her voice and could only talk in a whisper. For months I was the only one who could understand her over the phone. Slowly, with speech therapy and daily exercises, she built back some volume and a raspy facsimile of her once full-bodied voice.

During Mom's treatment and the initial months of her recovery, I was preoccupied with taking her to appointments and making sure she had what she needed. As her routine normalized and she needed me less, I thought more and more about the journal articles. What if she *did* only have one or two years left? The thought was unsettling. It wasn't just the end-of-life stuff that weighed on me. We had unfinished business with our relationship: the undercurrent of bad feelings we never seemed able to put behind us and that permeated all our attempts to be on closer terms. One or two years was not a lot of time to figure it out and make our peace. I would try to spend more time with Mom than before the cancer.

Mom alluded to her mortality on occasion, but she didn't let it stop her from living life as usual. I went with her to Home Depot to buy new rugs to replace the worn ones in her house, keeping my pessimistic thoughts to myself about why she should bother.

I started traveling with her, taking her along on my road trips to Southern California to visit Andy's family and my kids who were down there for college. When those trips turned out to be manageable, I booked flights and hotel rooms for us to visit Mike in Virginia, and an old family friend who had moved to Mississippi.

I told Andy and Mike I had figured out the secret to traveling with Mom: "Make sure you *over*-communicate the plans and details of what's going on, even if she's right next to you hearing the same information, and be extra patient when she's packing or getting ready to go somewhere."

Both responded with some variation of, "You mean, give in to her need for attention and treat her like a child?"

They weren't exactly wrong. I managed to head off her typical bitter assertions about what a burden she must be and how no one really wanted her along, but it cost me a lot of upfront mental effort.

In the meantime, she went in for regular PET scans to monitor for new growth. The scans came up clean time and time again.

A couple of years after the radiation treatments, too soon yet to call the cancer in remission, I realized the success of our travels was not all my doing. We were on a walk around the lake near her house when she shared her reflection.

"I have good days and bad days. But even on the bad days I still have food to eat, a bed to sleep in, and a roof over my head. I have so much to be thankful for. Even if I die tomorrow, I've had a great life. My kids and grandkids are healthy and doing well. Maybe they don't call me all the time, but that's okay. Nobody's in prison or on the streets—what more could I want?"

My ears perked up, as this was not a sentiment I was used to hearing from Mom. Acceptance? Contentment? Actual gratitude? The cancer had given her a new perspective on life. Maybe this was a turning point in our relationship. I murmured affirmative phrases, trying not to let my hopes show so I wouldn't break the spell.

We went on another trip in 2016, the biggest one yet: a Rhine cruise followed by a week in Germany visiting Mom's remaining friends and family. Although it was a successful and fulfilling trip, she decided it would be her last to another continent; travel was stressful and she was getting old.

Mom's thyroid cancer did mark a turning point in our relationship. In the six years since, she's been more grateful and less demanding, and I've been more accommodating and less defensive. The email battles have ceased; our communication is no longer tainted by sniping and negative vibes. Now I see our time together as an opportunity rather than an endurance test.

And yet. We never had an actual reckoning—an airing of grievances and coming to an understanding of past hurts. It's only been a cease-fire. A cease-fire I'm grateful for and that I'm not going to take a chance of undoing by confronting Mom directly. But I do want to understand our old relationship dynamic and why it was so thorny and persistent.

I also want to understand Mom better as a peer. What would I have thought of her had I met her as an adult? Could we have been friends? What kind of person is she, really? I couldn't see her accurately through the haze of our emotional baggage; my sporadic investigations of the psychology and self-help sections of bookstores and the early internet had not yielded clarity over the years.

Now, after six years of peace and a few weekends of downsizing, I'm ready to rekindle my search. I just need some inspiration.

SIX

The Books

June 2019

On Weekend 4 of downsizing, we tackle Mom's collection of over a thousand books—the size of a small library. "It's getting harder for me to read," she says, referring to the macular degeneration that makes things in the center of her field of vision look fuzzy. "And when will I even find the time? It's all I can do these days just to take care of my basic physical needs. Most of my books can go—I don't need them anymore," she says with a wave of her hand.

For the first few hours, we make excellent progress. She makes two piles—a big one to give away and a much smaller one to keep—and I pack them into boxes. She's willing to part with most of her now-outdated law and work-related reference books, and the books on sociology, history, and politics she continued to amass after completing her degrees in related fields: a bachelor's in political science and a master's in sociology.

The remainder of her collection covers a myriad of interests: nutrition and fitness; psychology, relationships, and self-help; music and spirituality; travel; popular fiction. And, by my estimate, eighty-something books on decluttering and getting organized.

As the day goes on, she slows down—it's getting harder to make decisions. I fix us an early dinner and she goes to bed soon after.

The next morning she's recovered some of her energy and we continue. At one point I notice the *keep* pile has become larger than the *donate* pile. Yesterday she wasn't sure if she would ever visit new places or try new recipes or learn new exercise routines again, but today she's practically manic as she argues with me, saying yes, I want that, to all the things she said no to yesterday.

"Did you go through these already?" I ask, scrutinizing a stack.

"Yes. I want to keep those."

I read aloud the title of the book on top: "*Beyond Mars and Venus—Relationship Skills for Today's Complex World,*" and give her an expectant look.

"Who knows, I still might meet someone. I'm only 83."

"What about these two that are about yoga—do you need both?"

"But they aren't the same." She points to the titles. "This one is *Spiritual Yoga* and the other is *Core, Pilates, and Yoga.*" I don't bring up the fact that she nowadays only does Fitbit steps at home and goes to Curves for directed activities. Who am I to discourage her from getting other forms of exercise?

"Surely you don't need this one." I hold up a book titled *How to Read Music*. "You've sung in choirs and played the recorder all your life."

"I can use it to teach my grandkids about music." True, spending more time with Andy's kids is part of the plan. Never mind that the book is written for adults—I can already hear what she'll say: "Oh, they're smart, they'll get it."

I pick up the next one. "*Weight Watchers New Complete Cookbook*. You don't use the Weight Watchers system anymore."

"But that book is a good one. I cooked a recipe out of there once and it was delicious."

"What about these two?" I hold up copies of *Making Peace with the Things in Your Life*, and *Sidetracked Home Executives*. "I've packed at least ten other books on organization that you're taking with you. You'll spend more time reading about getting organized than actually getting organized."

"But all those books have different approaches, and I won't know which one works for me until I try them out. One of these two may be the exact one I need."

And with that, I am done arguing. Mom's hoarding compulsion is in full force and my logic is bouncing off it like small pebbles. She'll probably never pick up any of these books again, I think as I pack them into the *keep* box.

Now she takes a closer look at the books in the *donate* pile. She retrieves a giant German cookbook from near the middle. "How will I ever make sauerkraut again?" she says and moves it to the other pile.

Damn. I didn't pack those away fast enough.

SEVEN

Preparing for Inspection

June 2019

I've been sacrificing my weekends and hobbies in my single-minded quest to get Mom's house ready for market. I missed out on my daughter-in-law's birthday party at a winery because it was on a Saturday afternoon and all scenarios led to losing a big chunk of my time at Mom's. I suspended my drum lessons, a just-for-me hobby I started after my divorce two years ago, because I can't afford the time to practice. But it's okay. I'm fully committed to the goal of helping Mom dig herself out of this hole of her clutter and getting her set up to enjoy her remaining years. Birthday parties, wineries, and drum lessons can resume when we're done.

It's a big job. We sort stuff all day long: keep, donate, recycle, or trash. I do most of the packing and stacking boxes and moving large things. Mom dusts and sweeps. People from Mom's church give us a hand by hauling away items for donation. They take hundreds of books, cassettes, and DVDs, most of her gardening tools and supplies, and several large pieces of furniture Mom is ready to part with. Like the queen-sized bed that sits so high that short people like us have to hoist ourselves into it. Mom hasn't slept in it for years—she prefers the daybed in the small bedroom. I sleep in the giant bed until it gets donated, then I'm on the uncomfortable fold-out futon couch. Mom no longer wants the three-piece sofa set, of which only the love chair is worn. The couch and stuffed chair, long under the protective cover of piles of stuff, are like new. Another casualty: the heavy, unwieldy, and outdated entertainment center that took hours to free from all the pieces of equipment connected by a web of wires in the back. The piano, on the other hand, she'll keep, because now she'll have time to learn to play it.

In addition to the physical tasks, there's the mental work of project management: the constant revisiting and updating of what must be done by when; having to call and interact with people to schedule services, review contracts, and arrange payments; and managing people's expectations. Tiring, but doable on most days—my twenty-eight years in the corporate world haven't been for nothing.

As for managing Mom's expectations, I over-communicate about everything and let her have as much input as possible. This works out well, mostly. Sometimes she needs extra persuading.

I tell Mom about a company I found online that specializes in large containers for moving and storage. "They'll leave one of those big rectangular metal boxes in your driveway. You can fill it at your convenience and let it sit there until you're ready to move or send it to a warehouse in Milpitas for storage and move it later."

"Why do we need that? We can just put everything on a moving truck when we're ready."

"There'll be a lot more room in here to move around if we can load up a pod with things that we already know you're taking."

She juts out her chin. "We don't need that—there's enough room." *Sure, I think, if I contort myself to maneuver between the piles and spend extra time moving things back and forth to create enough space to work in.* The idea of continuing this way is crazy-making.

I take a breath and try another tack that involves the realtor. "Remember Cindy wants to schedule a home inspection next month so we can get repairs done before putting the house on the market. The inspector needs to be able to walk around and have access to walls and electrical outlets. We should load up a pod the weekend before the inspection."

"Oh, he can find his way around. The people who work on houses, they're used to it. I had my kitchen and my floors done and nobody ever said anything to me about my stuff. They don't mind." But she lets me schedule a pod delivery for Weekend 8 after I tell her it can be cancelled without penalty if we call a few days before.

On Weekend 7, she tells me again that the inspector is a professional who knows what to do and that the pod is an unnecessary expense. Fine. I postpone the pod to Weekend 11, which will save her three weeks' worth of the container rental fee. By then she'd better be used to the idea, because I don't intend to give in again. Weekend 11 is only a couple of weeks before our target date of putting the house on the market, by which time we will need the inside of the house largely empty for staging.

This trend of staging houses to market them to potential buyers is, curiously, something Mom let us talk her into: "Well, if you think it's a good idea." Cindy advocated for it, and I supported it, thinking it would force us to get most of her things out of the interior living space by Weekend 13. For which we will obviously need a pod.

Or not. Apparently, I'm not thinking out-of-the-box enough. "The neighbors down the street that just sold their house, I saw them come back during escrow to start moving out. Their garage was filled to the top. We can just move everything into the garage." I groan inwardly and wrack my brain for more pro-pod arguments to convince her otherwise.

I share my apprehensions with Andy, who has a proposal: "I've been offering to come up there for a weekend to help out. We'll just tell her I'm coming up that weekend to help load the pod." And that's that—no more challenges from Mom about the pod.

Not so for the other recommendation made by both Cindy and Andy, who also works in real estate: Mom should move out of her house when it goes on the market because it will be easier for realtors to show the home to clients if no one is there to have to schedule around.

"Why should that be necessary?" Mom complains. "I'm a nice person. I won't bite anyone. I can go for a walk in the park while they show the house. Or I can take a mattress and go sleep in the garage and no one will have to see me at all."

I ignore this last suggestion and offer her the spare bedroom in my house. It will be a bit cramped, since my daughter is living with me to save money for a down payment on a place of her own, but the three of us should be able to manage for the week or two it might take to get an offer and go into escrow. Then Mom can move back into her house, and we should have at least three weeks to pack up her remaining things before escrow closes and it transfers to the new owner. Mom's living situation after that is still to be finalized. We've made a couple of trips to Orange County where we explored condos in a gated 55-and-over community and visited a senior living facility near Andy's place. We have another trip planned in late August to visit more places and pin things down.

But first I need to convince Mom to stay with me while her house is on the market. We go back and forth about it for several weeks, but finally I hit on the right word. "A couple of weeks at my house," I tell her. "It'll be like you're on vacation."

"Well, how can I resist that offer?" For the remainder of the weekends she makes jokes about packing for her vacation.

After Weekend 7, Cindy emails the real estate contract for us to review and Mom to DocuSign. Mom calls me during the week, apoplectic. "What is all this now with the DocuSign—everything done on the computer! And when I print it out to see better, it's so small I can't even read it! What are they trying to do? Do they not want me to see what's in the contract?"

I make a printout and bring it with me on Weekend 8.

"Yours came out much better," she says, showing me her version with the tiny print that she sent to the printer in some roundabout way from preview mode. I show her how to get a proper printout and how to enlarge documents on her computer screen so she can read them; she takes detailed notes that she later loses.

Mom scrupulously reviews the contract on the legible paper copy. Then I walk her through the DocuSign process on her computer. Squinting, she selects the calligraphy for her electronic signature and scrolls through the document, clicking in the spaces that require her signature or initials.

"Why do they do it this way?" she grumbles. "What's wrong with paper? The computer companies just want your money. They want to take everything over!"

"That's the way real estate is done now. It saves everyone the time it used to take to mail or deliver things back and forth."

"It's so inhuman—everything on the computer. What about the people who don't have a computer? It's discrimination against poor people!"

We go through some version of this for every one of the seven or eight additional documents she has to DocuSign for the remainder of the process.

I spend the rest of Weekend 8 working furiously to get the house decluttered enough for inspection on Monday. Mom's job is to tidy up the small bedroom and clear everything away from the walls. I distract her a few times with questions about the cleaning products and toiletries while I clean the bathrooms, but other than that we work separately. At some point on Sunday evening, I look up and notice the time. I'm late getting our dinner assembled, usually a salad with a protein and healthy crackers that we eat around 7 p.m. I walk into the kitchen to find Mom hunched over the sink doing dishes.

"It's 6:40. Should I get started on dinner?"

"I don't know," she mutters into the sink. She stops scrubbing, turns her head slightly in my direction, and says more loudly, "I have to do the *dishes*. And you're so *busy*."

I feel like I've been punched in the gut. I take a breath and keep my voice neutral and light. "Are you hungry?"

"*Well*," she says, turning back and scrubbing at a spot, "maybe I'm not *allowed* to be hungry."

My mind races. What could I have done to upset her? "Are you irritated with me?"

She turns and looks at me, surprised. "Oh, no, no," she says with utter sincerity. "Not at all. You're an angel. You're working so hard and getting so much done, and all of it for me." She turns back to the sink and scrubs some more. "I'm mad and disappointed at *myself*. I had one job this weekend and that was to get the small bedroom done. And what did I get done? Nothing. Just look at it—it looks the same as before."

Now it's my turn to be surprised. And it's not at her lack of progress.

I'm stunned to find myself open to the idea that her sarcastic barbs hadn't been aimed at me.

EIGHT

The Accents on Words

1963 -Present

When I was a child, I paid extra attention when Mom started stressing syllables while talking, because this meant she was mad, and it was my fault. She didn't have to yell to get the point across. She stretched her lips to show her teeth and hissed her sharp words at me, eyes boring into my skull, until she got the reaction she wanted, and then a switch flipped and everything was sunshine and rainbows. It had been like this for as long as I could remember, all the way back to my earliest memory.

I don't remember what my crime was, exactly. It could be I spread out my toys and Mom tripped on one. I might have snickered.

She looked at me hard and made her lips thin. "*Du* findest das *lustig*. (*You* think that's *funny*.)"

"Nein, Mami." I shook my head and looked at her shoes.

"Das *gefällt* dir aber—deiner Mutter zu zeigen wie *dumm* sie ist. (You *enjoy* that—showing your mother how *stupid* she is.)"

My chin was trembly. I picked up a block and put it in the toy bucket.

"Ja, so ist's gut. (Yes, that's good.)" She sounded a little friendly again.

I put another piece in the bucket, and another, until none were left.

"Siehst du? Das ist doch viel besser, hm? (See? That's so much better, hm?)" I didn't look at her face, but it sounded like she was smiling big.

She came close to rub my back. I bent down to get away from her hand and looked at the wall. I wanted her to go away.

She made tsk-ing sounds with her tongue. "Ach, du armes Ding—hast solch eine böse Mama." ("Oh, you poor thing—you have such a terrible mother.") Then she walked away.

There was a pattern to our interactions. One element was the suddenness of her irritation. There was no warning, no explaining of rules or what she wanted, no chance for me to correct my behavior in the moment. Another element was the lack of clarity about my transgressions. Her words were short on the specifics of what I had done, centering instead on accusations about my thoughts and intentions: "*You* think I'm *stupid*." "*You* did that on *purpose* to show everyone what a bad *mother* I am." "*You* just want to get a *rise* out of Mama."

I was not conscious of such thoughts and felt

unjustly accused. But part of me worried she might be right: the kernels of resentment I felt could be a sign that deep down I was petty and mean-spirited and unworthy of love. Whether I deserved it or not, there was one thing I was sure about—Mom was disgusted with me. She'd leave the room and slam the door only to come back again and again as she thought of more things to say about how hateful I was. Sometimes she disappeared into her room and bawled loudly through the closed door, as if to prove her point.

I built up an internal database of these scenarios to find the offending patterns in my behavior, but there was never enough information to prevent the next attack. Complicating matters was the occasional delayed reaction: saying I liked my grandmother's desserts seemed harmless enough at the time, but Mom brought it up later as evidence that her cooking wasn't good enough for me. I guess she had her own internal file of things I had said or done, which I tried to keep small by keeping my thoughts and feelings to myself.

The last part of the dance was in some respects the worst. After Mom felt better, she'd act like nothing happened and then make loving overtures. When I refused to respond, I was the one who looked sullen and difficult. "I *knew* you could do it. Isn't that nice?" delivered with a sunshiny smile and stroking my back like a pet, just seconds after belittling and shaming me into doing something she wanted. Or bragging about me in front of others: "She's such a good daughter—she babysits for me so I can go to school. She's smart and talented, too.

It's so wonderful to hear her play the piano!" Behind closed doors I heard something different: I was a mean, unloving daughter, but not to worry—she would take all the responsibility for raising me that way, since she must be a horrible mother.

So, which was it? Was I a good daughter or not? Maybe it didn't matter. To Mom's face I was obedient: I did my chores, babysat, went to church, and got good grades. Behind her back I did what I could get away with: I shoplifted candy bars from the local liquor store, smoked cigarettes with the at-risk kids in the corner of the field during lunch break, and made out with boys I hardly knew. Most of that stuff she never found out about, but when I was thirteen, I got black-out drunk after my friend and I snuck a bottle of whiskey from her mother's liquor cabinet. Apparently, I cursed like a sailor and threw up and scared my friend enough to make her call her mother at work, who then came home and was worried enough to call mine. Mom grounded me for four weeks. To my surprise, she withheld her venom during that time; it almost felt like she cared about me.

After I completed my punishment, it was back to business as usual. I made myself as small a target as possible, but sooner or later she talked to me with sharp edges again and I felt vile. Emotional gouging, I came to call it—talking in a way that inflicts the most hurt.

I held out hope that this was normal parent-child friction and that we'd have a better relationship after I moved out, but we didn't. I also couldn't figure out what our arguments were about.

I decided to ask her during one of them, thinking if we could identify the real problem then we could fix it with logic. It didn't work. She denied being upset and dismissed my suggestion that there was something she wanted from me.

"I don't know what you're saying. I've never had anything but love for my children. But it seems they don't feel the same way about me," she said, pained and triumphant.

I had no idea what to say next. I sure wasn't going to tell her I loved her too.

In my late twenties I learned about conflict resolution in a training course at work. I was excited: here was a systematic approach to address our fighting. Apparently, I hadn't been using the right words. The next time she was displeased with me and started making accusations, instead of saying, "Why do you always assume the worst about me?" I reworded it in the recommended format:

"When you say I enjoy watching you fail, I feel hurt because it seems like you think I'm a bad person."

She thought for a moment, then said, "What about *my* feelings?"

And we were back to square one: her feelings and all the ways I was failing her. So much for conflict resolution.

When I was in my early thirties, Mom started seeing a therapist.

"Is it because of our communication problems?" I asked.

"No," she said, "it's because of you."

I caught my breath, then asked in a calm voice what she meant by that. She started rehashing the same old complaint: she'd shown me nothing but love and I wasn't returning it. I cut the conversation short.

Not long after, I initiated an estrangement. "What's the point of our relationship if we're always upsetting each other and making each other unhappy?" No more visits, no more phone calls; cards were okay. Mom asked if I was sure, but she didn't argue. And she abided by my conditions.

Andy tried to talk me into reconnecting with Mom. "She's blood," he intoned. I declined. It was so nice not to have to think about her and her needs. I didn't miss her at all.

After a couple of years, Andy engineered a scenario to get Mom and me face-to-face. He was coming to the Bay Area for a brief visit and didn't have time to see us separately. It worked. Mom was gracious and charming, and our old conflicts seemed far in the past. Bit by bit, we began talking and making plans to see each other again.

Sometime the following year, Mom brought up the subject of our relationship. She sounded different after a couple of years of Prozac and talk therapy. "I feel like there's a distance between us—we're not as close as we should be. I get the impression you're holding something against me. Is it because I made you babysit your brothers?"

I nearly laughed out loud. "No, I never had a problem with the babysitting." I thought carefully about my next words. "It's just that you seem angry at me a lot of the time."

She looked at me intently. "I don't understand why you say that. What am I doing that makes you think I'm angry?"

My heart was thumping. We were having a calm and rational discussion, and I didn't want to blow it by saying the wrong thing. "It's your choice of words, and your tone. It's sarcastic and kind of bitter, like you're mad at me."

"My words and my tone," she repeated slowly. "Can you give me an example?"

I thought for a moment. "Do you remember when you apologized for giving birth to me? You said you must be such a terrible mother since I don't treat you with the same devotion you show your own mother."

She looked puzzled. "Yes, I remember saying that. But I wasn't using angry words, and my voice was low. And my face wasn't frowning."

What? Now *my* face was frowning. That statement had been full of hate and daggers, I thought. But all her *not-angry* boxes were checked: she hadn't been loud or frowning and there were no angry words directed at me. I couldn't think of a response, so I tried another tack.

"What about when you make accusations? You say I enjoy seeing you fail or that I want bad things to happen to you. It makes me sound like a horrible person. Do you really think I'm like that?"

"Well, I don't know what you're thinking. You never tell me anything."

"So . . . you don't necessarily believe those

things. You just say them to see how I'll react? To find out what I'm thinking?"

"Yes," she said with conviction and a bit of something that sounded perversely like pride.

"Why don't you just ask me what you want to know? Accusing people of stuff makes them uncomfortable."

"I don't know what you mean by that. Someone is uncomfortable if they have to sit on a hard chair or if the room is too hot."

Suddenly I felt light-headed. Was she messing with me? It felt like we were on different planets. I couldn't come up with a level-headed response, so I suggested we continue the discussion another time.

I mulled our exchange to figure out what had gone wrong. Maybe I hadn't been clear enough about my grievances. When we picked up the conversation again, I provided more examples of times I'd felt hurt, in excruciating slow-motion detail. She was bewildered. She denied any animosity on her part and more than once told me I shouldn't feel that way because that's not what she intended. I found this more disturbing than comforting.

Toward the end of our next session, she said, very sincerely, "I'm sorry for the things I said in the past that were hurtful to you." She offered me her hand with a gleam in her eye: she had reached out and listened and properly apologized, and now we could put this behind us and have a close relationship. I knew she had no idea what she was apologizing for. I predicted she'd continue to lash out at me and act as if I had nothing to feel bad about. I took her hand and shook it.

In the ashes of my disappointment was a glint of something to salvage: our Rational Discussion had provided me with new information to research.

I knew Mom could be very literal. She'd wrinkle her nose at someone's choice of food and point out how much fat or sugar was in it, then claim it wasn't a criticism because she never said the word "you." Or she'd rail at somebody, then insist she wasn't trying to influence them because she hadn't specifically told them to do anything. I always thought she was playing innocent so she wouldn't have to apologize and could continue with such behavior. Something similar appeared to be going on now with the way she was denying awareness of her own anger and of others' emotional discomfort and pain. But what I found odd was her willingness to take me through her reasoning, which was crude and simplistic: you know if you're angry by your facial muscles, making accusations is an acceptable (or even clever) way to find out people's thoughts, discomfort is only a physical sensation. Could it be she really saw things this way?

I would use the World Wide Web to investigate. We'd gotten access on our desktop computers at work a few years before, in the late '90s, and I'd taken to spending my lunch breaks at my desk surfing the net. I found good chemistry sites that were helpful for work, but the topic that really drew me in was psychology—what made people think and act the way they did.

I discovered the DSM, the Diagnostic and Statistical Manual of Mental Disorders.[1] One of the sections was about personality disorders, in which a person has maladaptive and rigid patterns of thinking and behaving that cause them problems, but they blame those problems on others because they see nothing wrong with their own thoughts or actions.

The first personality disorder that drew my interest was paranoid personality disorder (PPD), characterized by pervasive distrust and suspicion of others to the point of interpreting their motives as malevolent. Mom with her paranoid accusations checked all the boxes, but I checked a few myself. Criterion number 3 read, "Is reluctant to confide in others because of unwarranted fear that the information will be used maliciously against them." Mom certainly found ways to use my own words against me, so I didn't think my fear was unwarranted. But I supposed people with paranoid PD would say the same thing.

The cluster B personality disorders came closer to accounting for Mom's emotionality. They include narcissistic, histrionic, borderline, and antisocial PDs, and are characterized by difficulty regulating emotions and behavior, leading to actions others consider dramatic, overly emotional, or erratic. It wasn't long before I came across the online message boards. You could join a group and post about your experiences and get support from others in real

---

[1] American Psychiatric Association, *Diagnostic and Statistical Manual of Mental Disorders*, 4th ed. (Washington, DC: American Psychiatric Association, 1994).

time. These were not professionals but everyday people who used everyday language to describe their relationship difficulties and provided their laypeople's advice to others. I joined a couple of groups for the significant others of those with cluster B PDs, and it was cathartic. I immediately resonated with the pain and confusion of the online posters and eventually added comments of my own under the pseudonym Dandelion.

After a while, I was sated. And I began to feel I was barking up the wrong tree. The online posters described a deviousness and destructiveness that I never saw in Mom. She didn't sabotage us (or herself) when it came to physical survival. She made sure we got an education and knew how to take care of ourselves so we could go out into the world and be independent. Whatever her disregard for our emotional state, it didn't affect her genuine caring about our health and safety and financial stability. When it came to the concrete things, I had to admit she was a conscientious parent. And wasn't that what mattered? At some point I abandoned the idea that Mom had a personality disorder—I wasn't sure she met the DSM criteria of the maladaptive pattern causing problems across a broad range of social, occupational, or other important areas of functioning. As far as I could tell, her problems were just with her close relationships. Or just with her children, since she did have close friends. Or maybe it was just me that got riled up by Mom's behavior.

Andy's advice was to let it slide like water off a duck's back. When Mom started with her shenanigans, he would walk away, telling her, "I'm willing to have a discussion about this but only if we can talk like reasonable adults." She didn't understand what he meant, but I noticed she was more restrained around him than me. Mike was more confrontational. He tackled Mom's refusal to ever admit being wrong about anything by pointing out examples of her often-contradictory arguments. This resulted in her declaring she deserved to be loved, not criticized, even if she was wrong. I didn't have Andy's ability to disengage or Mike's mental fortitude. What I had was endurance. And curiosity.

After my Rational Discussion with Mom, I approached the Yahoo search engine with new terms: *trouble understanding emotions, emotionally unaware, emotionally blind.* I was rewarded with the word *alexithymia*, which translates from the Greek as "without words for emotions." The term was coined in 1973 by psychiatrist Peter Sifneos to describe a striking inability of many of his patients to articulate their distress or to explain why they acted in certain ways.[2] People with this trait have trouble identifying or describing their emotions—they may have the normal physiological responses associated with an emotional reaction, but they don't properly map onto a conscious feeling state that helps them interpret what's going on. Like Mom deciding whether she's angry or not based on a few externally observable criteria. The difficulty alexithymic individuals have interpreting their own emotions extends to problems recognizing emotions in others and navigating emotional interactions in

---

[2] P.E. Sifneos, "The Prevalence of 'Alexithymic' Characteristics in Psychosomatic Patients," *Psychotherapy and Psychosomatics* 22, no. 2 (1973): 255–262.

general. According to psychiatry professor Graeme Taylor, "the presence of alexithymia is likely to both initiate conflict and intensify ordinary developmental conflicts."[3] I felt validated: here was Mom's behavior, described and named by professionals.

Alexithymia affects about 10 percent of the general population,[4] with significantly higher rates in those with mental health conditions such as post-traumatic stress disorder, eating disorders, depression, and autistic spectrum disorder. Since alexithymia is not considered a stand-alone diagnosis, I considered each of those possibilities for Mom. PTSD sounded like a stretch since Mom's stresses and irritations seemed generic and not related to her wartime experiences. Her eating habits appeared within normal bounds, so nix on the eating disorders. Depression? Mom's therapy included treatment for depression, and she did seem better now—less prone to irritability and lashing out. But the alexithymic traits—the rudimentary way she talked about emotions—were more obvious now than before. This made me doubt her alexithymia was associated with depression.

That left me with autism. I knew a bit about it, as I had discovered it around the same time as the personality disorders. Autism is a neurodevelopmental condition that affects people's social skills, some to the point of not being able to communicate

---

[3] G.J. Taylor, R.M. Bagby, J.D.A. Parker, "The Alexithymia Construct: A Potential Paradigm for Psychosomatic Medicine," *Psychosomatics* 32, no. 2 (1991): 153-164.

[4] K. Honkalampi et al., "Why Do Alexithymic Features Appear to Be Stable? A 12-Month Follow-Up Study of a General Population," *Psychotherapy and Psychosomatics* 70, no. 5 (2001): 247-53.

verbally.[5] I hadn't given it much weight, since Mom had impressive social and verbal skills. She could talk circles around me, and she charmed other people like nobody's business. She wasn't always logical or straightforward, but she knew how to get what she wanted. From people, and from life in general. She was educated and accomplished—she had raised three kids as a single mother while going to school, and now she was a lawyer and owned her own house. That didn't sound autistic to me—it sounded powerful and in charge.

I looked into it anyway. I found a few first-person accounts by individuals on the autistic spectrum. They had succeeded in school and at work because of their ability to hyperfocus, but many aspects of ordinary life were a struggle. Out in the world they were drained by their interactions with people and by having to constantly figure out unspoken social rules. Once home, they were too mentally exhausted to deal with simple day-to-day tasks; they developed hacks and shortcuts for meals, laundry, and cleaning, and let the rest go. The nonautistic people in their lives didn't understand why they were so fatigued and reluctant to socialize. Apparently, autistic people could be educated and accomplished and pass for normal in the outside world. But the rest of it didn't sound like Mom. She had a system for getting housework done, piles of stuff notwithstanding, and plenty of energy for socializing.

Further reading took me to a concept called

---

[5] Uta Frith, ed. *Autism and Asperger Syndrome* (New York: Cambridge University Press, 1991).

theory of mind. This refers to the ability to construct internal mental models of other people's thoughts and motivations, an important skill in social interaction. Most people learn this intuitively during childhood, but many autistic individuals have trouble with it.[6] This sounded like it could apply to Mom, although it wasn't straightforward to connect the dots. The fact that she didn't know what was in my head wasn't surprising, since I was so guarded around her. But if her accusations were meant to get information out of me, wouldn't she choose the most likely ones, to see which made me flinch? It was true I had negative thoughts about Mom, but they didn't resemble her accusations. Gloating or provoking her was the furthest thing from my mind—I was usually preoccupied with keeping her in a good mood.

I recalled an incident in a different context that seemed like it could be a theory of mind issue. Mom's front door was next to a full-length window that had no curtains or blinds. When she was alone in the house, she occasionally puttered around half dressed. If she was doing something in the kitchen or TV room, she was in full view of anyone who approached the front door. During the day it was harder to see inside, but I came over one evening after dark and was horrified to spy Mom through the window in her underwear, illuminated in her

---

[6] S. Baron-Cohen, *Mindblindness – An Essay on Autism and Theory of Mind*, (Cambridge: MIT Press, 2001); M.A. Neff, "Autism and Alexithymia: Similarities, Differences, and Overlap," *Neurodivergent Insights* (blog). neurodivergentinsights.com/blog/autism-and-alexithymia. Current thinking associates theory of mind deficits with co-occurring alexithymia rather than with autism per se.

habitat like an exhibit at the zoo. Mom shrugged off my concern: "If someone comes to the door, they can look away if it bothers them." Mom was inside her own house minding her own business. It wasn't her intention to make a spectacle of herself, so no one was going to see her that way.

Maybe autism wasn't so far-fetched. But where to go with this information? Certainly not to Mom. Broaching any of this with her was out of the question. We had a conversation once about public schools and their mandate to teach kids with special needs, and she commented that the autistic children are the ones who can't communicate with others. How in the world could I tell her I thought she might be autistic? The very idea of it exhausted me. What would be the point, anyway? She was in therapy, and it was helping. Let the therapist bring it up if it were legitimate.

I did, however, run it by my brothers. They were the front-line witnesses to our upbringing, and it was important to have them vet my findings. Each had his own slant on Mom's behavior. Mike believed she had a psychological need to control others; he was fascinated by her mind games and power plays. Andy didn't care about the whys and took a behaviorist approach: he'd be a dutiful son as long as she behaved herself, but if she started acting crazy, he was out the door.

Neither of them bought my theory about autism, for all the reasons I had doubted it myself. Mom was socially adroit. She could be sweet and charming when she wanted to ingratiate herself with others, or manipulative and punchy when things didn't go her way. As for her disorganized house, well, that was a choice. She could make the time to work on it by cutting back on her socializing and hobbies: singing in the choir and playing the recorder; hiking with the Sierra Club; getting involved in church, clubs, and local politics; gardening; and traveling. Perhaps they were right. Heck, I couldn't get my house organized either. And I was less socially at ease than Mom. Maybe I was the one with autism. Hoping to salvage a shred of my theory, I told them about alexithymia and then recounted the Rational Discussion I had with Mom in which she'd shared her unusual ideas about emotions. But something got lost in translation; they didn't know what to make of it.

I dropped the idea of autism, but not entirely. For the next decade, I kept my eye out for evidence that Mom processed information differently, including emotions. Progress was slow since we didn't get together often. I was busy with my career and raising a family, and she was busy enjoying her retirement, visiting her aging parents in Europe, and dealing with her first bout of cancer. Every so often we had another skirmish, and I noodled the new clues, but I didn't know where to go from there. I still had to contend with her anger whether she acknowledged what it was or not. And I still didn't know what I was doing to bring it on. Keeping things light and positive and not reacting to her negative comments had always been in my repertoire, and that's what I continued to do.

In the new peace that followed Mom's thyroid cancer in 2013, I no longer had to contend with her unpredictable anger. By that time I was making fewer assumptions about her, communicating more explicitly, and becoming less frustrated when she didn't behave as I expected—all to good effect. By the time we started downsizing in 2019, our relationship was on good footing. I was still curious about how her mind worked, but this was no longer driven by the need to predict and manage her next outburst.

Things went more or less smoothly until the hiccup in Weekend 8 when she threw sarcastic barbs at me because *she* hadn't gotten enough done. It was hard to imagine her angry sarcasm wasn't targeted at me; the accents were, as usual, expertly placed for maximum effect. But this time I was receptive to her explanation.

I went online after I got home. A search on *speech patterns in sarcasm* led to the word *prosody*, which refers to the rhythm and stressing of syllables in spoken language to communicate beyond the words. Prosody can signal emotions and attitudes such as intent, emphasis, irony, or sarcasm.

A search on *disorders of prosody* turned up autism spectrum disorder (ASD), among other conditions. Difficulty understanding and using prosody in social communication occurs frequently enough in people on the autistic spectrum that it is considered a characteristic.[7] Hmm. It had been almost two decades since my last internet foray into autism. Maybe it was time to give it another look.

The landscape looked much different. There

---

[7] R.B. Grossman et al., "Lexical and Affective Prosody in Children with High-Functioning Autism," *Journal of Speech, Language, and Hearing Research* 53, no. 3 (2010): 778-93.

were many more first-person accounts, including memoirs and celebrities coming out, a proliferation of advocacy organizations, resources, support, and educational material, and remarkable advances in neuroscience and therapeutic interventions. The tone had shifted from thinking about autism as a disorder or deficiency to be cured, to seeing it as a difference in the brain's wiring that was part of normal human variation, and that should be accommodated and even celebrated. *Neurodivergent* was the new term,[8] and included under its umbrella additional conditions such as attention-deficit/hyperactivity disorder, dyslexia, and Tourette's. The new picture of autism was a far cry from the early stereotypes, which held that autistic people were mostly male, that they were robot-like and lacked empathy, that they had unusual or obsessive interests and behaviors, that they weren't sociable, and that they were unlikely to have close relationships or families.

I constructed a scenario for the Weekend 8 incident. Mom was frustrated with herself for not getting enough done. If I played a role, it was to provide a contrast that made her feel inferior. She expressed her frustration in a way she knew from experience would get results. "You're so *busy*." "I have to do the *dishes*." "I'm not *allowed* to be hungry." This prosody—this way of talking—got people's attention because it sounded like sarcasm directed at them. Perhaps most were inclined to react in a conciliatory way, to smooth Mom's ruffled

---

[8] S. Baron-Cohen, "Editorial Perspective: Neurodiversity – a Revolutionary Concept for Autism and Psychiatry," *Journal of Child Psychology and Psychiatry* 58, no. 6 (2017): 744-747.

feathers. She would have felt better and not given it a second thought, unaware that some would come away with an elevated heart rate or a bad taste in their mouth. Of people who openly took offense at her sarcastic tone, she'd say, "Oh, they just don't like me."

I felt giddy with accomplishment. I had a working hypothesis: Mom was autistic with alexithymia. I could continue my observations for another couple of months to refine my theory. Maybe Mom and I could have a true reconciliation before her move to Southern California.

NINE

Memento

June 2019

As I observe Mom with her stuff, I try to think back—was she always this disorganized?

Early in the downsizing process I watched her go through a pile of mail in the living room that had been accumulating for several months. She picked up each envelope, took out the letter to reread it, and then, with few exceptions, put it back in the envelope and into the new stack she had created to deal with later. The result was maybe a 10 percent reduction in stack height. This made me uneasy—should I be concerned? Part two of this process came later when we needed to clear the area: "Oh, just put those stacks over there in that box. There's room." Then I discovered the boxes of papers dating back to the '80s. I was both horrified and oddly comforted; she's been this way for a long time.

She's made efforts to get organized along conventional guidelines. We find unopened packages of organizers for office supplies tucked away in drawers and boxes. Sticky notes protrude from multiple books on organization. There are handouts from seminars on how to organize your important papers that have her handwritten notes on them. She quotes the organizer mantra of *everything in its place* and laments she never set up a proper office after moving into the house twenty-seven years ago. But the filing system she came up with for her regular bills in the early 2000s looks like nothing I've ever seen: monthly packets consisting of a printout of her online banking statement wrapped around a small stack of the paid bills that show up on that statement, secured with a rubber band and placed in shoe boxes marked with the calendar year.

At least it's chronological. If there's no apparent reason for a given set of papers and documents to be together, it comes down to proximity in time. A manila envelope marked *personal and financial* contains the contract for having the roof done, drawings my kids made, and a handout from a political group she was involved with—a mini time capsule from 2006. Or there's an intention of being close in time: at the bottom of a stack of blank stationery are cards and letters she received years ago, still unanswered.

She buys in bulk and crowds her counters and surfaces with duplicates: paper towels, shampoos, lotions, other toiletries. "I leave those out, so I don't buy new ones," she tells me. When she finishes the next-to-last one of something, she washes out the empty container and puts it in a shopping bag in her car as a reminder to buy it again. This is because she loses her shopping lists, as evidenced by the old ones I keep finding in the paper piles in her boxes. I'm reminded of the movie *Memento* where the main character wakes up each morning with no memory of the day before. He writes himself notes at night so he can pick up where he left off; he gets the most critical information tattooed on his body. With Mom, this might be serving sizes of food—she portions hers out with measuring cups to maintain the right nutritional balance in her diet.

One thing not found among the clutter on the kitchen counter is the bottle of dishwashing liquid—this she religiously puts back under the sink from where I need to retrieve it every time I do the dishes. The sponge and dishwashing brush, however, can stay out.

She's excessively organized in certain ways. Paper wrappers from tea bags do not go into the recycling bin individually because it makes a mess; they go into an empty tea bag carton on the back of the stove that goes into the recycling bin when full. Empty protein bar boxes stay in the pantry until all the empties can be reassembled into the original multipack before recycling. She efficiently packs things into a bag or purse, filling every cubic centimeter, then unpacks half of it when she has to get something out.

And socks. She stops me from putting a stack of empty plastic produce containers in the recycling bin because she wants to use them for sorting her socks. I tell her the socks will take up more space that way, but she argues she needs to better see what she has. Okay. This isn't nearly as outlandish as her organizer notebook with one sock in each of the clear plastic pockets.

Mom is fanatical about eliminating water where it shouldn't be. She towels down the bathtub after one of us uses it. When I carelessly shake the water from my hands while preparing our dinner salad, she stoops down with a rag and dabs up the water droplets on the floor around me. Rinsed plastic and metal containers for recycling can't be put in the transitional paper bag next to the garage door until they're dry. She dries the dishes by hand, which seems to me an unnecessary waste of time when there is so much to do. I can't argue, though, that her obsession with drying surfaces has probably kept them in better condition—no water spots or dullness from hard water residue.

Throw rugs protect the floor in high traffic areas, and old towels cover the throw rugs to protect them. The towels are smaller than the rugs, so we constantly trip over the edges of the towels and snag them with chair legs as we get up from the kitchen table.

Mom complains the realtor didn't say anything about the nice wooden floor she had done in 2002. I try not to sound incredulous when I remind her that people can't see the floor when it's covered with stuff.

Mom seems to filter out the clutter when she's looking at her floor or her nicer things. She has beautiful little sculptures, pictures, and knick-knacks, but you have to concentrate to locate them in the sea of plastic figurines and containers, cheap souvenirs and saved string, and baskets of small items that don't go together. If someone points out she has a lot of clutter, she acts either sheepish or defensive: "Well, should I have not gone to college and educated myself? Should I have not gone to law school and had a career?"

She admits it looks better after I've cleared a few surfaces, but she can't follow suit. She stares at her things, the wheels turning sluggishly, trying to get her mind to work. She'd rather busy herself with hand-drying the dishes, getting a spot out of the tablecloth, or sweeping the footpaths throughout the house that don't need sweeping. None of these things relate to downsizing. No wonder she has no sense of where we are in the process or how something will affect the timeline. "Just imagine—I'll be out of this house in a month," she says, relying entirely on me to make it happen.

That doesn't stop her from getting bent out of shape when I can't give her an exact date for something, or when dates get shifted around, which is par for the course in the real estate business. She can't put a plan together to save her life but then challenges every aspect of the ones I make. "Why are we doing it this way?" "Why can't I do what the neighbor did?" "That's not what I remember from the '70s when we sold our first house." She's not arguing, she says, just trying to understand.

Really? It feels like she's coming up with every reason she can think of *not* to do it the way I've laid out and making me work to convince her otherwise. And then she forgets something we've already resolved and starts the same line of questioning all over again. But if I threaten to let her take over a task, she backs off and says, "I don't always make the best decisions." This is exhausting, and it's taking a toll on me.

She mentions that her blood pressure has been lower lately, in the normal range. "How is yours?" she asks.

"I don't know," I lie. In fact, it was unusually high a couple of weeks ago at my last wellness check-up at work. It seems we've traded blood pressures.

That's not to say Mom is lazy. She's highly detail-oriented and has an elaborate system of rules for daily tasks that takes all her time and keeps her from getting more complicated things done. She works diligently when I'm there on the weekends telling her what to do, but she can't manage the simple downsizing tasks I leave for her during the week. She doesn't have rules for those, so she falls back on what she knows: workouts at Curves, lunch at the senior center, trips to Costco and Trader Joe's followed by the ritual washing and repackaging of all her produce. Laundry is an all-day affair, as is going through the mail and paying the bills. God forbid there's a haircut or dental appointment—that can keep her busy for days catching up on all her other chores. In the end, she's not making any decisions about her stuff while I'm away. This is a continuing thorn in my side.

She's always had excuses for not getting organized: hobbies, depression, working full-time, dealing with cancer. Each valid enough to give cover, yet none currently in the picture, including depression. At the time of her cancer diagnosis six years ago, she had been lowering her Prozac dosage for years, saying she didn't think she was depressed anymore. She then dropped the Prozac entirely to focus on the cancer and never looked back. Now it's her hunched back she threw out over a year ago and her worsening macular degeneration that keep her from making more progress. Right. But I should cut her some slack. She does have a bad back and bad eyes. I should be grateful she can still do all the things she's doing.

Online, I find a term for this over-reliance on familiar and detailed rules: *hyper-systemizing*.[9] Systemizing refers to figuring out the rules for how things work. According to British clinical psychologist Simon Baron-Cohen, "the systemizing mechanism is set too high in people with autism. As a result, they can only cope with highly lawful systems and cannot cope with systems of high variance or change (such as the social world of other minds)." Or with big and complex projects such as downsizing.

Still, I'm surprised how little she's able to contribute. Working side by side, I see significant problems with planning, time management, working memory, and cognitive flexibility. These are executive function issues.

Executive function is an area of difficulty for up to 80 percent of those with autism.[10] But another

---

[9] S. Baron-Cohen, "The Hyper-systemizing, Assortative Mating Theory of Autism," *Progress in Neuro-Psychopharmacology and Biological Psychiatry* 30, no. 5 (2006): 865-872.

[10] M. Bennie, "Executive Function: What Is It, and How Do We Support It in Those with Autism? Part I," Autism Awareness Centre, Inc., March 19, 2018 autismawarenesscentre.com/executive-function-what-is-it-and how-do-we-support-it-in-those-with-autism-part-i/.

cause of executive function problems is dementia, a progressive loss of intellectual functioning due to changes in the brain.[11] Old age is the biggest risk factor. About a third of 85-year-olds have some level of dementia,[12] and there are usually signs of cognitive impairment before the symptoms become obvious. Mom is 83. Could she be in the early stages of dementia?

I keep asking myself if Mom's organizational issues were always this bad, and I feel relieved when I find evidence that they were. Otherwise, they might be associated with dementia rather than autism.

When I was growing up, there was always clutter, and we were always late for church and school events. Another clue comes from Andy, who helped Mom with her last three moves between 1987 and 1992: "I don't remember her ever sorting through anything before she moved to the next place. Everything got packed." On the other hand, Mom managed to pay the bills and keep a roof over our heads, assigned us regular chores, and saw to it that our health and schooling needs were met. She was organized and systemizing in some ways, but not in others.

The more I think about it, the less sure I am about why Mom can't help more with the downsizing—whether the project is too complicated for her autistic brain or if she's getting dementia. Maybe nothing's changed, and she's just been in her

---

[11] The website for the Centers for Disease Control and Prevention; the "About Dementia" page. cdc.gov/alzheimers-dementia/about/.
[12] I. Skoog et al., "A Population-Based Study of Dementia in 85-Year-Olds," *New England Journal of Medicine* 328, no. 3 (1993):153-158.

house so long she ran out of room to put things. Or she's gotten worse. Which could be early-stage dementia, or just tiredness from getting old.

I suppose it doesn't matter right now—the organizing falls to me either way. We'll see what happens in a few years.

TEN

The Tupperware

July 2019

On Weekend 9, I assemble all the old Tupperware I've found in various places: the back of a kitchen cabinet above the fridge, a storage cabinet in the garage, inside a large suitcase I've pulled down from the rafters of the garage. The Tupperware is decades old, some of it warped and sticky. Mom hasn't used it for years, having long ago wised up to the evils of plastic and switched over to glass storage.

Yet she hesitates to turn the lot over to me.

"Will you use any of them at home? Maybe I can take them to the senior center. I left some other plastic containers there last month and people took them."

We agree that she'll pick out the better pieces and their matching lids for the senior center and I'll take care of the rest. I leave her sitting on a stool in a sea of Tupperware on the family room floor while

I busy myself with the wall hangings and pictures.

A half hour later I hear her walk up as I'm taping together a cushioned stack of the larger framed pictures.

"I feel so guilty."

"Why?"

"Do you believe I'm a Christian?"

"Yes."

"I don't know anymore."

I stop and look at her. "Do you mean because you've accumulated so many material things?"

She looks away. "Jesus said we should give away what we have and follow him. I haven't done that at all." She is silent for a moment. "When we fled our home after the war, we took barely anything with us, only what we could carry in a small suitcase."

My mind drifts to the sepia-toned family portrait I rescued from a box of papers last week. A six-year-old girl with a big forehead and short curly hair stands between her seated parents. Her head is slightly cocked, and she looks out from the picture with an air of boredom or defiance, her hand perched loose and uncommitted on top of her mother's. A two-year-old boy leans back on his father's lap, seemingly comfortable there, though the real story was that he'd thrown a tantrum earlier about having to sit on the lap of this stranger who'd gone off to war two months before he was born. A hint of a smile plays on the father's lips, although everyone else wears a straight face in the style of the times. On the father's sleeve is the insignia of a corporal in the German army. This photograph, taken during a furlough, is the last one Mom has with her father in it. Shortly thereafter he left for Stalingrad and was never heard from again, presumed dead. Germany lost the war two years later, and the sizable German population living in Eastern Europe was expelled.[13] In a mass migration to the west, people took what possessions they could onto overcrowded trains, encountering violence and brutality along the way in retaliation for Nazi atrocities. Mom was nine, her brother five, my grandmother thirty-one when they left what is now Poland for Allied-occupied Germany. They searched for friends and relatives, bartered possessions for food, and slept in a ditch at one point. After reaching safety and reuniting with family in what would become West Germany, they rebuilt their lives, enduring suspicion and disdain from the local population as the massive influx of refugees exacerbated existing shortages of housing, jobs, and food.[14]

It's not a stretch to imagine this would lead to an obsession with material things. "I'm sure your war experience has something to do with it," I tell Mom.

"Do you think so?"

"Yeah."

---

[13] Wikipedia, Wikipedia's "Flight and expulsion of Germans (1944-1950)" entry, Wikipedia's entry on the flight and expulsion of ethnic Germans from Eastern and Central European countries at the end of World War II. en.wikipedia.org/wiki/Flight_and_expulsion_of_Germans_ (1944–1950).

[14] Peter Gatrell, "The Problem of Germany's Post-War Internal Refugees," *Literary Hub*, September 20, 2019. lithub.com/the-problem-of-germanys-post-war-internal-refugees/. German expellees are often referred to as refugees, although the legally correct term is internally displaced people.

"Thank you," she says, and goes back to the Tupperware. Ultimately, she collects a couple of bags of matching sets to take to the senior center. I take the rest home and dump most of it in the trash. Goodwill no longer takes it, and the internet says Tupperware that's old enough not to have a recycling logo, even though made of virgin materials, is likely to be sorted as trash at the recycling center.

While I'm well aware of Mom's accumulation tendencies, I continue to be surprised at the things I find. On top of older washcloths and hand towels in the linen closet, there are a dozen identical newer sets which she must have bought after I helped her organize it all those years ago. Nine frying pans in a kitchen drawer. Twelve cans of tennis balls. Not twelve *tennis balls*, but twelve *cans* of three tennis balls *each*, that she wants to pack and take with her, because "you never know." I pull out twenty-five vases from the cabinet above the kitchen sink, spreading them out on the floor, and ask which ones she wants to keep. "All of them. Each one is a little different." With coaxing, she selects seven for donation. Throughout her boxes of papers are dozens of never-activated credit cards, some of which have *activate* scribbled on the envelope. Two large crockpots, two clothes irons, multiple tape recorders, ancient stereo systems, a mass of computer equipment—she buys new gadgets because they have new features but keeps the old gadgets because they have the old features.

Mom asks me to exchange some lightbulbs in

the house with brighter ones she's bought. She comes back with a worn and dusty paper shopping bag and holds it open for me.

"You can put the ones you took out in here."

I look inside. It's half full of old bulbs. "Do all of those in the bag still work?"

She doesn't know. We have other things to do that day, so I put the bulbs I just removed in the bag—a sorting project for another day.

Back in Weekend 1, she showed me a recent advertisement for a Topsy Turvy tomato planter.

"It would be so easy to take care of. What do you think?"

"No," I said. "Didn't you tell me your basic self-care takes so long that you barely have time to watch the news on TV? Why add one more distraction to get in the way of the huge task ahead of us?"

She held out the circular to me. "Maybe you'd like to get one—it's such a good deal."

Weeks later, working my way through years of accumulated stuff in her garage, I brush the dust off an unopened box containing a Topsy Turvy tomato planter.

By Weekend 10, my patience is wearing thin. She isn't doing any decluttering while I'm gone. Every weekend I come back to the same landscape of stuff covering the same surfaces. Today I see the beginnings of a new stack: mail order catalogues freshly culled from the incoming mail.

"No," she insists, "I'm not buying more stuff—I just like to look at the pictures."

And there's another new item. On the

windowsill next to the brick-and-board shelf is a mason jar of water holding a giant cactus paddle, no doubt from the plant outside. I try to ignore it at first, but then it sticks me as I reach for something on the shelf.

"Why is *this* here? We need to *clear* surfaces, not put more unnecessary stuff on them."

She puts on a sad face. "So, you want to throw him out?"

I fix her with my stare. "Are you going to take *him* with you?"

"Well, no. Okay, you can do what you want with him."

I wait until she's in the other room, then dump *him* in the green waste bin in the garage.

We don't have a specific agenda today, so she asks me what she should do. I go around the house and collect all the little containers with random bits and pieces in them. Paper clips, erasers, keys to unknown locks, cough drops, coins. Broken plastic and metal and ceramic pieces from unknown gadgets and housewares, tiny rubber gaskets, ear buds. Tiny floss packages, gift ribbons, old half-burned candles and tea lights, mini flashlights, nail clippers, rubber feet to something, hair clips, small mending kits, dice, expired credit cards, mini cassettes, plastic tokens, little velvet pouches, old business cards, dusty seashells, luggage tags. Campaign buttons, regular buttons, cancelled stamps, pencil stubs, rubber bands, string, springs from old pens, stickers. Whistles, keychains, broken jewelry clasps, tiny perfume packets, and an incense holder.

The containers cover two-thirds of the kitchen table. "You can sort those," I tell her.

In the meantime, I tackle a giant box full of toiletries I found in the master bedroom. It's filled with old half-used and congealed cosmetics, travel-size shampoos and soaps, unused Mary Kay cosmetics and marketing materials from the '70s, hair clips, first aid supplies, sticky dust, insects. Empty little jars and bottles, both washed out ones and the kind you can buy empty. Four curling irons and three sets of hair rollers. Gadgets to give you a massage or physical support or that apply heat. As with everything else, there is nicer or brand-new stuff interspersed with the old and broken: an almost full bottle of Nivea lotion, boutique shampoos, lotions, skin toners, unused gauze and cotton balls, unopened fancy soaps and perfumes.

We work at our respective tasks all day, taking a break at noon and clearing enough space on the table to eat lunch. I come into the kitchen again around 6:30 to get started on dinner and ask her how it's going.

She laughs and nods at the detritus in front of her. "I certainly am learning my lesson. Are you trying to punish me?"

Maybe, I think. *Quite possibly.* I smile at her and say, "It needed to get done. Better you than me."

ELEVEN

My Father

1931 - 1992

At the end of World War II, my grandmother, (Oma) Martha, and her two young children lost their home in what is now Poland and joined the mass exodus of Germans fleeing to the west. Oma Martha found a place for them to stay in the Russian-occupied zone of Germany, working as a house-keeper for a rural German family in return for room and board. Several months later she heard from the Red Cross that some of her relatives were further west in Osnabrück, in the British-occupied zone. She packed up the kids again, and they went to reunite with the family. Through the Evangelical Free Church in Osnabrück, Oma Martha found a room and board arrangement in nearby Fürstenau. One of her duties was to care for the woman of the household who was dying of cancer. Oma Martha stayed on afterwards and eventually married the widower, who became Opa to me. They moved a couple of times after that, but I only remember their last house in Steinau an der Straße, a picturesque town in the German countryside that's known as the hometown of the Brothers Grimm, who collected and published German folktales in the 1800s.

My favorite part of visiting my grandparents as a child was Oma Martha's cooking. The most enduring memory I have of Oma Martha is in an apron, bending over an assemblage of ingredients and implements on her small kitchen counter. I especially loved the cakes and pastries we had for Kaffee und Kuchen every afternoon. I did not care for the Mittagsschlaff, the mandated nap after the large midday meal. I would either lie awake bored or fall deeply enough asleep that I missed out on the afternoon treat.

In addition to her talents in the kitchen, Oma Martha could catch flies with her bare hand. She tried to teach Mike, but his success rate was only 10 to 20 percent compared to her 90 percent. Opa Herbert was round and gruff with white unruly hair and earwax. But he had a twinkle in his eye when he called me "die kleine Dunkle"—the little dark one. While I inherited my mother's stocky German frame, the darker complexion came from my father.

My parents met on the street in Frankfurt in 1959. Mom was working as a secretary, chafing under the sexual discrimination and harassment that was rampant in the '50s, and still bitter about her younger brother being able to attend university while she was told no because they couldn't afford it. Dad was good-looking, with brown skin and a nice smile, and he cut a dashing figure in his suit and tie and combed-back pompadour. He was from East Pakistan (now Bangladesh) and was working odd jobs while figuring out how to get into one of the vocational schools for textile engineering. His family back home was relatively well off, but the two older brothers who controlled the money did not support him in this endeavor. They had sent him to the University of Calcutta, but he was an unmotivated student and had trouble finding a job after graduation. One day he didn't come back after taking some of the family's livestock to sell at the market—he went west with the proceeds in search of better opportunities. Once there, he was on his own, although his sister sent money on occasion.

Dad's German was bad, so he talked to Mom in English; she responded in German so he could improve. They had things in common. Both came from farming families and had left behind homelands undergoing geopolitical upheaval. Both had a rebellious streak and felt like outcasts. To her delight, he talked politics with her, something she couldn't get other men to do.

Their relationship went against the traditional expectations of both families, not just culturally but religiously: she was Christian, and he was Muslim. Oma Martha, a devout Baptist, told Mom, "Das kannst du uns nicht antun" ("You can't do that to us"). But Mom could be immovably stubborn when she thought something was right. That, and she believed she'd eventually convince Dad to convert. They were married in a civil union with her brother the only family present. Many years later she told me, "One of my regrets in life is that I never had a proper church ceremony." A black-and-white photo shows them on the steps of the courthouse, a long bouquet of flowers across her arm. She is pale and slightly plump, in a tailored dress suit with her short hair styled in loose curls. He is thin, dark-skinned, and slightly taller, wearing a loose-fitting suit typical of the era, his hair in a pompadour showing off his widow's peak. Once they were married, Oma Martha developed a mantra she recited whenever his name came up: "Er ist ein guter Mann" ("He is a good man").

It wasn't long before problems started. Mom put Dad through vocational school, figuring he would get a steady job and she would stay home to raise a family. He flunked out and told her he didn't want children. She persuaded the school to let him repeat the training and poked a hole in her diaphragm. Once I was born, he fell in love with me. I was also responsible for revoking her pariah status with her family, so excited were they that I ate and cried and pooped like a normal baby. But I didn't fix all the problems. Dad did only a little better with the training the second time around. Mom implored the school to give him the vocational certificate since he was close to passing, which they did on the condition that he not apply for a job in the area. So, it was back to odd jobs.

He was gentle with me and took me for walks. When Mom berated me, he stuck up for me, just a bit. He'd tsk and furrow his brow and say to her, in his heavy accent and a pleading tone, "Du mußt nicht so mit ihr reden (You don't have to talk to her like that)." This enraged her—she was the one doing all the work at home—and Dad backed off. His intervening didn't have much practical effect, but I got a taste of what it felt like to have someone in my corner.

I didn't notice any obvious friction due to cultural or religious practices. Mom had extracted a promise from Dad that I would be raised Christian, and he did not interfere. Nor did he try to teach me Bengali or impart much of his culture. He wore a lungi at home—a tube of fabric tied at the waist to make a skirt covering the legs. Occasionally he made curried chicken with green beans or cauliflower, but more often it was made by Mom who had learned the recipe. A few times I saw Dad eat a meal the traditional way—scooping up rice and sauced meat or vegetables with his cupped fingers—but only in the presence of Bengalis who were doing the same. Mom didn't mind this or the occasional visits from the Bengali relatives, but she was annoyed when Dad slipped into his native tongue and forgot to translate for her.

They separated in the late '60s. He took off with her savings and started a business venture back home, only to find she would not, under any circumstances, move us to a Muslim country to join him. Dad's older brothers offered to set him up in an arranged marriage if he stayed, while Oma Martha tried to fix Mom up with a German guy. All for naught, as Dad returned (without the money) and Mom took him back.

Andy was born a year later. I was at home with

Dad when the hospital called with the news. I didn't understand why Dad started hooting with laughter and doing a little dance around the phone. "Ein Junge!" ("A boy!"), he finally shouted at me.

When I was eight and Andy almost one, Dad received a job offer after doing some contract work in the US, and we emigrated from Germany to Southern California on Green Cards. Two years later, Mike was born, and Dad was fired from his job.

Dad sued for breach of contract. "They are discriminating against me. It's against the law," I heard him say over and over, and I believed it with a child's righteous indignation. Sometimes I overheard the term *insubordination* when he talked to Mom or his lawyer—apparently that was something the other side had made up so they could discriminate against him.

Working odd jobs again, he moped around the house, self-absorbed in his lawsuit. Mom and Dad fought constantly and about everything. She berated him, yelling, while he frowned and shook his head. One day, when I was eleven or twelve, he slapped her across the face.

"Ruf die Polizei an!" ("Call the police!"), she shouted at me.

I was in shock, transfixed.

"Geh ruf die Polizei an!" she yelled again.

I was nauseous. I didn't want to do it—I was on his side.

Dad came to my rescue. "Don't bother her," he told Mom. "I will go." He went to their bedroom to gather a few things while Mom hurried to the phone and called the police. Dad was gone by the time they arrived. They made a report and left.

Not long after, Mom filed for divorce. I was glad: now there would be less fighting, and Dad could live in peace.

We had to sell the house. Dad made just enough to support himself and make sporadic child support payments. Mom moved with us kids into subsidized housing and collected food stamps and AFDC—Aid for Families with Dependent Children. Dad lost the lawsuit, and the one after where he sued the first lawyer for malpractice. He came over every weekend to take my brothers and me out for junk food, to the beach, or to the video arcade. I wasn't into video games and resented that my brothers got to waste all those quarters playing Pac Man; I bristled when Dad let them cheat at mini golf. But then he pressed a twenty into my palm when he dropped us off at home and all was good. He brought us over a few times to the apartment he shared with John, a skinny young Vietnamese man who wore big sunglasses and smoked cigarettes. One of those times, Dad made us curried chicken that was so spicy I could only eat a small piece on a big pile of rice.

Seeing Dad was a treat if only to get away from Mom for a while, but I couldn't altogether stop the internal eye-rolling at his fatherly advice:

"Finish your education, then life will be easy."

"Be careful about the coffee—don't drink too much."

"You should take garlic—put a clove in each cheek and chew on them. Good for health." Dad did smell a little pungent at times. I hadn't realized it was the garlic.

But not everything he said was corny and benign.

When I wanted to get my ears pierced, he said, "Why you want to do this?" His tone was gentle, not critical.

"I want to wear earrings."

"You are making holes in your body, and they will be there for the rest of your life."

"That's okay."

"You don't need to do it. There is no reason you have to."

I was silent.

"Think about it. Then you can make your own decision."

This confused me: I'd already made my decision, and I wasn't swayed by Dad's arguments. But the idea that I could think for myself lodged in my mind and grew, giving me permission over the next couple of decades to figure out more complicated problems on my own. By the time I was truly thinking for myself and became curious about his thoughts and decisions, he was gone.

I was in graduate school when Dad had a heart valve replacement; he had been getting winded due to heart damage from childhood rheumatic fever. After the operation, he began taking Coumadin, a blood-thinning medication he would need for the rest of his life to prevent blood clots. He lived for a few more years, long enough to see me get my doctorate, land a corporate job in the Bay Area, and present him with his first grandchild. Leah was almost two when we got the call from the emergency room doctor in Anaheim. Dad's roommate hadn't been able to wake him that morning. He'd had a stroke, and most of his skull was filled with blood—an intracerebral hemorrhage. (I would find out later that Coumadin can interact with certain herbal supplements, including garlic, and cause bleeding.) The hospital staff waited for Andy and Mike to get there to say goodbye before taking him off the ventilator. He was sixty-one.

Mom and I both lived in the Bay Area at the time, as she had relocated to be closer to her new grandchild. We caught a flight to Southern California the next morning. After the funeral, the four of us drove to the house where Dad had been renting a room so we could clear out his things. Other than the furniture that we left with the landlord, we had the entirety of Dad's belongings loaded into one of the vehicles in a matter of hours. Those things eventually ended up at my place since I was the oldest child and legal next of kin. I donated most of his clothes but kept his good suit and shoes. What remains of his worldly possessions fills six medium boxes in my closet, waiting for a time I can go through them more carefully—vocational records, legal depositions, medical reports—to round out my picture of who he was. Maybe when I'm done with Mom's downsizing.

TWELVE

The Pod

July 2019

During lunch on Weekend 10, Mom barrages me with questions.

"What time do you think Andy will get here on Friday night? Do you think he'll want to have dinner? Should I buy salmon to make for lunch? Do you think he'll want my bed and we girls can sleep in the other room?"

When she's done with those, she has more.

"Do you think we'll be done in three weeks? Why does Cindy say we need to be done in three weeks when the stager has five weeks in her contract? When am I coming to live at your house? I need to figure out when to do the laundry. How am I going to get my mail and pay my bills when I'm not here? If I move out at the beginning of August, I won't get the Master Card or the water bill because they come later. How long do I have to stay with you?"

These questions are important—Mom needs to keep herself organized. I answer as many as I can and look forward to the end of lunch, when I can go back to interacting with inanimate objects.

On the following Friday, the pod is delivered to Mom's driveway, and Andy drives up from Southern California in his pick-up truck. He's persuaded me to have my kids come over to help while he's here; one of my sons is also bringing his girlfriend. This is something I've been avoiding—it's easier to interact with Mom on my own than to find suitable tasks for everyone and mediate the process. But they arrive on Sunday morning with coffee and bagels and get to work helping Andy muscle the upright piano into the pod. It's remarkably heavy for its size, but they manage to have it only gently drop down the step while maneuvering it out the door, and not on anyone's foot. The tie-down straps didn't come with instructions. Andy and I watch YouTube videos to make sure we ratchet them properly to secure the piano. After moving the rest of the furniture and boxes that are ready to go into the pod, the millennials order pizza and beer on somebody's smartphone and bring it back to eat at the picnic table in the park next door. Andy joins them while Mom and I sit inside and have our usual microwaved salmon, steamed vegetables, and pouch of quinoa and brown rice from Costco.

Mom brings up the stager during our meal. "Have you seen the photos on her website?"

"No."

"There's so much clutter in them. It's horrible. Why should I work so hard to get rid of my clutter and then pay her money to bring clutter back in?"

"I'll take a look at the website," I mumble. I

worry that Mom will want Cindy to find us a different stager, but, as quickly as she brought it up, she backs off.

"Well, Cindy knows what she's doing. If Cindy trusts her, I will, too."

When Mom goes to lie down for her post-meal nap, I join the group outside and suck down one of their beers.

After lunch I point the kids in the direction of the boxes and give them sorting guidelines. Mom doesn't object. She knows they'll see personal stuff and things might get purged that she would have kept, but by now she admits she can't do it herself and expresses her appreciation for their help. I, on the other hand, am hovering.

"It's okay, Mom," says Leah. "Go do other stuff."

"Yeah, Mom," says Nathan. "We got this."

"We won't throw out anything that looks important," says Nathan's girlfriend Ash.

"We'll let you know if we find anything of interest," says Nick.

They spend the rest of the afternoon sitting cross-legged in the living room and sorting papers in the sweltering summer heat because the air-conditioner isn't working. But they have fans blowing on them and playlists playing in the background, and they're talking and laughing and enjoying themselves. Mom and I regard the scene with amazement. Why hadn't we asked for their help earlier? They generate a record amount of paper to recycle, filling up not only Mom's recycling bin but most of the backseat of my car, including the footwells.

Andy cleans up around the outside and in the garage, tears out the cheap storage cabinets installed over the toilets, and fills his pick-up with two loads of junk and old equipment to haul to the dump. He organizes and ties down everything inside the pod, which ends up only half full, to my chagrin. I'd predicted we'd fill this one up and would need a second one for the rest of Mom's stuff. This was because I'd drawn my packing layouts in two dimensions, ignoring how much could be stacked in the third dimension. We'll send this pod to storage and retrieve it for the final packing instead of ordering a second one. A significant savings—Mom will be happy.

When I get home, I take my measuring tape out to the car to estimate the volume of paper I just transported: about 14 cubic feet, which translates to 635 pounds, or the equivalent of 3.2 average-sized men or 3.7 average-sized women, according to the Centers for Disease Control and Prevention (CDC). No wonder my car scraped the driveway. I fill my 96-gallon recycling bin as high as I dare, about two thirds full, or the equivalent of 2.0 men, and jerk it to the curb. The remainder goes in after it gets emptied on Monday.

This weekend couldn't have gone any better. Having Andy and the kids help made a huge difference. We might just make the target date after all.

THIRTEEN
Almost Showtime

July 2019

"We're making good progress," I tell Cindy after Weekend 11. "Still shooting to have the house ready for market in two weeks, but it feels like there's a lot left to do. Worst case we might need another week."

"It should be fine to list a little later in August. When is Todd coming to do the repairs?"

"This weekend. He says they should be able to get everything done in a day." The inspection after Weekend 8 had turned up a couple of termite infestations, water stains on the ceiling, and dry rot on outside wood.

"That's great. He'll do a good job for you at a reasonable price—I've used him a lot." Cindy's reassuring manner does not quell my reservations. Todd came over last weekend to look at the things we wanted him to fix, showing up more than four hours late. The next day he emailed me a picture he took with his phone of a handwritten itemized quote on a generic invoice form—no contractor's license number, no mechanic's lien notice, no contract to sign. It came to $800 less than the inspection company's quote—he was all about saving us money. He wanted half up front, requesting I send a check made out to him to his home address. I googled him and found he was an employee at a legitimate construction company. The work on Mom's house is clearly a side job, which makes me leery. But Cindy trusts him, and we trust Cindy. Mom is okay with the amount and lets me handle the arrangements. I send Todd a personal check, adding it to the running total of costs for which she'll reimburse me.

The termite treatment must get done before the weekend, so Todd can replace the termite-damaged wood. We'd been working on this since getting the inspection results almost three weeks ago. It would have been a piece of cake to coordinate the treatment through the home inspection company, but Mom had used a different termite company for those same two infestations almost two years ago, and it was still under warranty for one more week after the inspection. Andy offered to contact them and arrange for retreatment under the warranty. On the Wednesday afternoon following the inspection, he called me from the road.

"The termite company says they can do the retreatment at no charge, but we need to pay for them to come out and do their own inspection—they can't use the one from the other company. It's $295."

"That seems worth it. It's less than the treatment estimate from the inspection company."

"That's what I was thinking. The other thing is, they need that reinspection payment by the end of today to keep it under the warranty. I don't have time to deal with it—I'm on my way to somewhere for work."

I offered to take care of it, thinking it would be a quick task. I was transferred from one person to another and had to explain each time how I was involved since they were already dealing with Andy and Mom. The final transfer was to a lady in accounting who was to take my credit card information, but the call went directly to voicemail. I left a message to call me back, but they were closing in an hour. I waited and fretted and called back several times until someone got us connected, and we got it done. Good thing I had no work meetings scheduled that afternoon.

The following two weeks were no less convoluted. The guy who did the reinspection told Mom one of the infestations wasn't active and she'd get a report. After hearing nothing for a week, I checked with Andy. He remembered getting an email from them that he hadn't opened. They'd sent it only to him and were waiting to hear back about scheduling the retreatment of the remaining infestation. Andy called and got it scheduled for Tuesday, four days before Todd is coming to do the repairs.

I call Mom on Tuesday night. "Did the guy come

to do the termite retreatment?"

"Yes, he came. But he didn't do the treatment."

"Why not?"

"He said the infestation wasn't active. They'll send us a clearance report."

That's good news, I suppose. But how odd. The home inspection had identified termite infestations in the same places that were treated two years ago, but both were inactive. I take a closer look at the copy Mom gave me of the final report from two years ago. Treatment had been completed, with a recommendation that the homeowner have the termite pellets removed and the wood replaced where damaged. Hmm. If Mom didn't have this done, the inspector could have mistaken the old infestations for new ones. I ask her about it next time we talk.

"Did you have the wood repaired after the termite treatment two years ago?"

"No, I don't remember doing anything like that. The termite people took care of everything."

Well. That was $295 and half a dozen hours of time between Andy and me that we didn't need to spend. I close my eyes and take a breath. It's not that much in the scheme of things.

The other thing to get done before the weekend is to schedule all the services Cindy wants in order to get the house ready for staging and photographs: house cleaning, yard clean-up, light landscaping, and window cleaning. All need to be done next week to stay on schedule. Cindy's been slow to get back to me with vendor names and they're starting to book up. After a few anxious days I get a spot on everyone's schedule, and luckily Mom is okay with all of it. Continuing my lucky streak, I find someone to repair the air conditioner on homeadvisor.com. He comes that same evening and fixes the air conditioner for a reasonable price. What's more, he's nice to Mom. I leave him a glowing review.

On Saturday, Mom and I wait for Todd and his son, who also works in construction, to arrive. They are two hours late, and I have to contend with Mom's "Are they coming? When are they going to be here?" and her snarky remarks about how if she'd been a man, they wouldn't be keeping us waiting. I'm immensely relieved when they show up. I walk outside to greet them, and they go about setting up. Todd is a big guy with a beer belly and a booming voice. He barrels through the house, taking no notice of Mom who is sitting in the TV room. She looks at him sternly and says good morning in her raspy voice, which makes him slow down and return the greeting.

Todd paints over the stains on the ceiling of the master bedroom and bathroom without looking for their source in the attic (or sending his much slimmer and better-looking son up there). It's okay, I tell myself, he's Cindy's guy. If the buyer wants to do their own inspection and an issue comes up, we'll deal with it then. Todd and his son eat their lunches in the driveway and drink beers all afternoon while they work on the dry rot outside. I'm not surprised when Todd tells me they have to come back the next day to finish, nor am I surprised when they show up two hours late. By the second evening everything is done, mostly. Todd leaves me with paint to touch up a few places they didn't get to because "the brushes are dead," and takes $75 off the remaining balance. I sweep the driveway after they leave and find about ten nails.

Mom and I continue our downsizing activities while the repairs are underway. This is Weekend 12, and I'm finding it hard to tame my irritation. Everything bothers me, including the twinge to the right of my bellybutton that might be a hernia from helping Andy load the bookshelves into the pod last weekend.

    Mom apologizes for what she's putting me through yet continues to put me through more of it. I've assigned her to work on the two wicker baskets full of gloves that have been in the living room for years. Each time I walk past, she tries to engage me in conversation about them, which I short-circuit with brief noncommittal answers.

    "I bought these when I worked in Stuttgart. There's a rip here on the left index finger that needs sewing."

    "Oh."

    "These are old, but they still look good. Do you think they'd fit you?"

    "Maybe."

    "These belonged to my stepcousin. She didn't want them anymore." Mom tugs them on, stretching and bending her fingers to force them into the holes. "They're a little tight, but I can still wear them."

"Mm-hm."

"This one is missing a mate. We need to find the other one before we give them away."

"Okay."

"These aren't so great, but I can use them for cleaning." She puts them on to demonstrate.

"I see."

She settles on six pairs to keep. Then she asks me where to put them since many of her clothes are already packed away in the pod and more of them will be in transit soon.

I'm so tired of trying to find a place for everything. I break into a cold sweat after opening yet another shoe box of completely random odds and ends. I stumble upon a glass jar of bright green and white feathers that Mom kept me from throwing out weeks ago—feathers she had collected as they dropped from Andy's childhood pet budgie. Thirty-five-year-old feathers. She was going to spread them in the park next door and wash the jar to reuse, but here they still are. I toss them in the trash, jar and all, when she isn't looking, and cover them up with dirty paper towels.

The clothes hangers on the doorknobs are driving me up the wall. Some have clothes on them and some don't, some are curved and some have clips, but regardless, they are packed onto doorknobs where they bulge out and wait for me to bump into them and knock them down. I badger Mom about why these things are hanging on the doorknobs and if we can't hang them in the closet instead so they're not in the way. She gives me reasons: the clothes are easier to reach, or she's setting them aside because she wants to put them in a certain place or with other garments. But she relents and lets me put them in the closet. The next day things are hanging from the doorknobs again.

On Sunday evening, Mom says to me: "One more week and it will all be over."

The termite issue comes up again after Weekend 12 when Cindy asks for the clearance certification. I search back through my notes and emails. Didn't Mom say the termite company was going to do that? I prod Andy, who calls and finds out they have to come to the house again to reinspect and make sure the damaged areas have been repaired before they can issue the clearance. They come on Thursday and email us another inspection report the next day showing *no new findings*.

"Is this the Section 1 clearance?" Cindy asks in an email. Andy doesn't answer, so I read the eight pages of fine print trying to figure that out, since nowhere on the document does it mention the word clearance or certificate. In the end, I don't answer the email either. Andy and Cindy are the ones in the real estate business—why am I going through this with a fine-tooth comb? The topic never comes up again.

Things go well with the services at Mom's house, with one minor glitch: the door of the refrigerator doesn't close properly after the house cleaning crew cleaned the inside. Mom tries to fix it by putting the shelves on a different level, but now her back hurts and she's agitated. "Can you call them to come back and fix it, since they caused the problem?" We figure out that the door will stay shut if she puts a chair against it, so I convince her to wait for me to look at it on Saturday.

On Friday I need to do something about the papers I've been driving around all week in the trunk of my car. They have Mom's sensitive account information on them and need to be shredded. It's several boxes and paper bags full, too much for my little personal shredder, and Red Dog is too far away. I google *shredding services* which turns up very little in the way of price information. I take my chances with The UPS Store across the street from my work. The lady at the counter tells me it will cost $1.99 per pound. I have maybe twenty pounds, I think—can't be much over $40, maybe $50 tops. I empty the boxes and bags onto the scale, then feel the blood drain from my face as I see the $150 tab. Boy, was I sloppy with my estimate—that modest pile of paper was closer to seventy pounds. Other options flit through my head, but all involve half a dozen trips to lug everything back into the car, which I need to be empty before I head out to Mom's tomorrow morning. I pay the $150.

On Weekend 13, it's back to just Mom and me. The refrigerator is an easy fix—the vegetable crisper wasn't pushed all the way in. By Sunday afternoon we've done as much as we can, and I've moved the remaining clutter into the garage in semi-orderly heaps so prospective buyers can walk around.

We survey the inside of the house. All that's visible of Mom's things are a few pieces of furniture the stager will work around: the coffee and end tables in the living room, the dresser in the master bedroom, and the daybed in the small bedroom. Everything else is hidden away in cabinets, drawers, and closets, including the futon I've been sleeping on. It looks sparse and surreal—not like Mom's house at all.

"What do you think?" I ask her.

"Well, it doesn't have much furniture."

I double- and triple-check the lock box with the keys inside for the stager and for Cindy, then I pull the front door shut and lock it. We caravan to my house in Livermore, with Mom following me closely in her car filled with vacation suitcases, shopping bags of food, and a small crate containing half a dozen orchids.

Off we go to the next part of the adventure. And none too soon—I really need a break.

PART II

Forty Days and Forty Nights at My House

FOURTEEN

Making Room

Early August 2019

My daughter Leah is twenty-eight. After earning her degree and working in Southern California for several years, she landed a job in the Bay Area and accepted my invitation to stay with me until she was ready to get her own place. We share dinners on the patio, go wine tasting, and get massages at the local spa. When I tell her that Mom will move in with us during her transition to a retirement community, I'm not sure what to expect. Leah experienced firsthand how Mom could be during a family trip to Bangladesh when she was a college sophomore. But she takes it in stride. "I can always disappear into my room if necessary." She helps me get the spare bedroom ready.

On August 4, 2019, Mom and I lock up her partly-emptied and cleaned house in San Jose and leave it in the hands of the real estate industry to put on the market. Less than an hour later we arrive in our respective cars at my house in Livermore.

DOWNSIZING MOM

Inside, Mom surveys the small and modest guestroom. The futon couch has been folded out to make a bed and takes up much of the space; it's made up with sheets and blankets I had on hand, and they don't quite match. There's a chest of drawers, an old but functional desk, and several boxes of Mom's papers I brought over last weekend for her to sort while she's here. "Oh," she says, "this is very nice." She'll have to share a bathroom with Leah, but that's no problem. She'll stay out of the way in the mornings while Leah gets ready for her job in Walnut Creek.

My refrigerator is smaller than Mom's, and it takes a while to make room for everything we've brought over in the cooler. Mostly it's produce. Mom likes to wash her berries and repackage them in saved plastic produce containers lined with paper towels, such that one container turns into three. As she's explained to me multiple times, they keep longer that way. We'll also need to make room for her melons once she cuts them open. For the several days it takes her to eat an entire cantaloupe or honeydew, she places it cut side down on a small dinner plate to avoid using plastic wrap.

Fruit takes over outside the fridge, too. Mom's enormous ceramic fruit bowl, filled with pears, plums, apricots, grapefruit, and avocados, hogs my small kitchen counter. The plastic clamshell package with fourteen round compartments for apples sits in a plastic bin on one of the kitchen chairs, just as it did at her house. She bought the original from Costco a long time ago and has been refilling it with bagged apples ever since.

Mom puts fruit in her daily protein-powder-fortified breakfast oatmeal and eats multiple pieces of fruit for dessert after both lunch and dinner. She's plied me with her fruit for the last thirteen weekends, even buying organic in case that was my problem, but I never managed to put away even half of what she did.

Now at my house, she looks at the bananas on my counter. "Do you put your bananas in the freezer?"

"No," I tell her.

"Why not?"

"I don't eat them that way. And those are not my bananas."

She turns to Leah. "Do you put your bananas in the freezer?"

"No," says Leah. "I like them better fresh."

"When they start to get those brown spots, you can freeze them before they go bad. Frozen bananas taste just like ice cream."

Leah looks at the bananas. "I only see one brown spot. I'll eat them before they go bad."

I help Mom set up her computer in her room and connect it to the Wi-Fi. Shortly after I leave the room, I hear her talking to herself, loudly complaining about the Windows 10 operating system she's had for several months. I go back in and look over her shoulder while she gripes. "What is all this? There's too much stuff open. I don't want this—how can I make it go away? Wait, what did you do? Where? Where's the escape button?", all the while balancing her unwieldy ergonomic curved keyboard on her lap.

I'm not unsympathetic. The Windows 10 user interface is a big change from Windows 7 and nothing about it is intuitive. But Mom seems to take longer to learn complicated things. On our trip to Mississippi several years ago, we visited Mom's old friend who had become an avid board game fan. Yahtzee and Uno were no problem—Mom was already familiar with those, and she held her own. Then Mom's friend tried to teach us Settlers of Catan, a strategy game that involves building up communities and cities by acquiring and trading supplies with other players. Each turn is a multi-step process, with rules to follow and decisions to make. It's too much for novices to absorb all at once, but they learn by starting to play, helped by reminders and by watching the other players. This is what I did, but it didn't work for Mom. She couldn't retain even the most basic rules; each time her turn came up she had to be directed step-by-step from the beginning. Mom's friend found it amusing at first, then puzzling. Half an hour later we ended the agony and moved on to Boggle.

Dinner is a cinch to prepare—all three of us like big salads. We eat on the patio and make small talk about climate change and other current events. Later that evening I'm in the kitchen and Mom is going through some papers at the dining room table when I hear her pipe up. "I can't see what I'm looking at—there's not enough light in here."

I stop what I'm doing and go turn up the dimmer switch. Mom goes from squinting to scrunching her eyes closed and recoiling. "Well," she says, "now it's in my face."

I give Mom a map of Livermore that I've marked with the locations of the local senior center, CVS drugstore, and Trader Joe's. Now she can go places while I'm at work. She's particularly interested in the senior center where she can get low-cost lunches during the week. But she finds it disappointing. She shows me a paper copy of their weekly menu when I get home. "Look at all these fried things and heavy sauces and carbs—white noodles and white bread. And they only have fish once a week. The senior center in San Jose has more vegetables and healthy foods." Then she hands me a large Ziploc bag full of chocolate chip cookies. "They had extras of these, so I took a bag home for you and Leah." After dinner, Leah and I each have one and thank her. Some days later, with Leah's approval, I bring them to work and put them out for my coworkers.

Mom grumbles about having to park her car in the street. "At home I always park my car in the garage. Now it has to be outside, and it's exposed to the elements." This was true: whatever the state of her house, she always left room in the garage for her car. At my house, the garage is filled with clutter and my car sits in the driveway.

Several days into Mom's stay, I come home from work and notice her car is not out front. I'm concerned she's out driving around during rush hour, but then I find her inside the house.

"Where's your car?"

"I parked it down a side street under a shady tree so it's not in the sun. Do you think your neighbor will mind? Should I go knock on the door and ask if it's all right?"

"Is it right in front of their house?"

"Yes, but I think they park in the driveway. And there are other spots around them."

I consider going out to have a look, then decide I'm overthinking it. "It should be fine," I tell her as I get started on our dinner salads. "You'll probably be moving it every couple of days. And anyway, it won't be for more than a couple of weeks."

Things are going according to plan in San Jose. The stager came on Monday, the photographer on Tuesday, and Cindy listed the house on Wednesday. An open house is planned for both days of the weekend. Cindy won't be there, because she's going out of town on a backpacking trip, but she's having somebody from her office cover it and will send us the person's contact information before she leaves.

On Friday morning, Mom asks if I've gotten any emails from Cindy. "No," I shake my head. "She's probably already left on her trip. It must have slipped her mind." On the inside, I'm annoyed and even a bit panicky—what if the arrangements fall through and nobody shows up to run the open house? But I tamp down my anxiety and address Mom in a calm and reasonable voice. "It probably doesn't matter that we don't have the other realtor's information. There isn't any reason for us to call. Cindy will let us know how the open house went after she gets back from her trip." Mom looks satisfied with that reasoning.

On Saturday after lunch, I get out my computer to do some work while Mom starts to explain her strategy of always having access to crisp apples.

"You can buy a whole bag of apples, and they'll keep for weeks," she says with a satisfied smile.

"Mm hmm." I find the presentation I need to work on and open it.

"All the apples in the bag fit exactly into the plastic tray. With one spot empty." She points to the one she's eating. I've heard this before. I smile at her and nod and then turn back to my slides. There's a pause of about twenty seconds.

"Of course, you're welcome to have one of these apples if you want."

"Thank you." I keep my eyes glued to the computer screen and try to focus. There's another extended pause filled with chewing sounds before she continues.

"This one is still nice and crisp. And only slightly sweet."

My mind is now completely blank. I nod again in anticipation of more apple lore, but she has nothing more to say. She gets up and throws away her apple core, then walks in circles to complete her 250 Fitbit steps before retiring into her room for her afternoon nap.

A few days earlier, I had retreated into my room with my computer, and she pursued me through the closed door.

"Daniela?"

"Yes?"

"Are you in there?"

"Yes."

In the end I had to come out and deal with her request anyway. I decided I might as well be a sitting duck in the common space while she was awake, if I wasn't going to be left alone when I was in my room. But the other option might have saved me from small talk about apples.

On Sunday, my sons and their significant others come over to join us for a dinner of family favorites: grilled salmon, corn avocado salsa, rice, and sangria that we enjoy out on the patio. Mom tells them the story of the war, how her father went missing in action, and how the rest of the family became refugees. They've never heard the story in this much detail and are rapt. I have a feeling of déjà vu. A generation ago, it was my Oma who was captivating a different audience with that story.

FIFTEEN

Mom's Retirement Speech

2001

When Mom invited me to her retirement luncheon eighteen years ago, it seemed a big enough deal that I took time off work to go. The celebration took place at a restaurant in San Jose near her workplace at the State Compensation Insurance Fund, or SCIF.

Shortly after I arrived, she pulled me aside and showed me a two-page printout of the speech she was planning to give. She had practiced it but was nervous about being able to recite it from memory. I assured her it would be acceptable to read from the printout. And so she did, standing before an audience of about forty of her co-workers, her eyes never leaving the papers that trembled in her hands.

Hello Everybody,

Thank you so much for coming today. I am

touched and moved to see how many friends I have. I really wanted to have this meeting closer to Independence Day, because I wanted to describe to you my life-long quest for independence. I know—I am supposed to keep this light and funny, but I hope you will allow me an exception. Today I would like to tell you a little more about my life's journey.

Usually, when people hear my accent, they ask me: Where are you from? This is a very friendly question, but not that easy to answer. And now that you have known me for more than 10 years, I will make an effort to tell you why.

As you know, many Germans have immigrated to this beautiful country over the years. And many Germans have immigrated to other countries. So when Katarina the Great called for German settlers, many of them came. I can only speculate that my father's ancestors followed her call and settled in the Ukraine. My mother's ancestors settled in West Prussia, which belongs to Poland today. After WWI it was also called the "Korridor," when it was given to Poland to have access to the Baltic Sea. As I was born to German parents, I remained German. After WWII the German Government pledged by contract with other countries at least 2 times that Germany never will attempt or ask for re-possession of the lands where I was born. Today, I am a US citizen, but the country of my origin on my Naturalization Certificate is listed as "Poland." However, I never was a Polish citizen. Does this sound complicated? It does to me, although I am quite familiar with the situation by now.

Shortly after I was born, my parents decided to

move closer to the "real" Germany and bought a little piece of land near Danzig, which today is called Gdansk. Up to 1940 our life was hard, but quiet. But 1940 really was not a good year for us. The first thing that happened also turned out to be the most devastating. In March my father was drafted into the German army. And no, he never was a member of the Nazi party. He was a gentle, quiet man who loved his family and became fodder for the war machine. After a short visit in either 1941 or 1942, he was sent to Stalingrad. We now know that only very few German men made it back alive. We were among the few who even received a notice of missing in action. But that was the last we ever heard of him.

Then, in April of 1940, a month after my father was drafted, my grandfather passed away. In addition to the personal loss, after that, there was one less person to mind the little family farm.

Finally, in May, my little brother was born. This normally is a joyful event. But now our family was quite helpless. This was the rest of us left: My grandmother, little me, and my mother with her little baby son. We got some help from neighbors whose men had not been drafted into the war. This was very hard for all of us, but somehow, and don't ask me how, my mother managed.

But the worst was still to come. And that was when the war action moved closer to Danzig. For a long time, I could not talk about it, all I wanted was to forget. Still today, I would rather tell you about the highlights—if you want to call it that—of that part of my life. Let me tell you I know what it feels like when grenades and artillery are going over your house from 2 sides, and after each time you check whether everybody is still breathing. I know what it feels like when the infrastructure is down, when you have to get a bucket of water or whatever one could carry from miles away. And everybody who had legs to walk had to pitch in and carry as much as they could. And one day you return "home" and the house where you lived is on fire and you have to either live in a ditch or find an empty house to stay. I have seen the effects of famine. Our little family was among the lucky ones—we had some food every day, even if it was only a slice of bread. Those were the days and months when I learned to pray. And to thank God for every minute we survived. We were fortunate enough that we were left with as much as we could carry (and some of it was bartered for bread) on our way to Berlin, where my mother thought she had some friends. When we got there—and don't ask me how— all that was left was rubble. No friends, no place to stay. My mother with her 2 little children just followed the road to the west. By today's standards, we were homeless. From then on, we were Germans alright, but we were called "refugees," something like a minority in a German country that was occupied by the Allied forces. Finally, my mother found a family farm where they would let us stay in return for my mother's work. However, we still were "refugees" for a long time to come.

That was when I started my quest for independence. I figured if I could manage to be as educated as possible, I would survive. I managed to get into secondary education in Germany. I wanted to become a teacher. But then, when I saw first-hand how teachers were treated by teenagers in general, I lost my confidence. Suddenly, to earn my way as soon as possible seemed to be so much more important. Well, that went fine for a while, until I fell in love and got married. This was a decision which again totally changed my life. I sure learned quite a few new skills, like making a husband happy and changing diapers. And having a husband and 3 children around brought me a lot of happiness and enjoyment. But I definitely had strayed from the path to independence.

Then something really exciting happened: My husband found employment in California. Pretty soon I found out that I had the possibility to go back to school. And I went. All the way through law school. By that time it was "sink or swim," as my husband and I had decided to part ways. When I finally was finished with law school, my daughter was married, and my son Andy went to Berkeley. A few years later my son Michael started to study history at UCLA.

After I passed the California Bar Exam, another exciting event occurred: mother SCIF took me into her arms. Looking back, that was the best thing that ever happened to me. Of course, I had to give up some independence, but what an opportunity to learn! I learned a lot about myself, things that I never knew before! In addition, it was a time for me to heal from the ravages of WWII. A few years after I started work at SCIF, I was able to take up a loan to purchase a pre-owned home. So finally I am not homeless any longer. I still miss my father. He would be 90 years old today. It would be so nice to tell him in person: Look, father, I am ok now. I do not have to worry about getting food any longer, and I have a roof over my head. Well, I still can ask my Heavenly Father to pass on this message.

Some of you have asked me: What will you do now with all your free time? Friends, I tell you: That is no problem. Finally I have time to take care of the things that I have neglected before. I have time to count my blessings. I have time to see more of my family—one of the reasons we have this celebration late is that I spent about 2 months with my mother and stepfather in Germany. And I am happy that I have children here in the United States, at least today. My son Andy, who has been a police officer and peacekeeper for the United States, is here. He came from Kosovo to spend Christmas at home. My daughter Daniela who normally takes care of her husband, a two-story house, her 3 children and full-time employment as a senior research scientist at the chemical department of a major American company, took time off from work to be here today. My son Michael is busy finishing his Master's Degree in History in Sacramento. I have grandchildren, whom I would like to get to know a little better. I have time to visit with my friends. I enjoy music and nature. I believe between that and taking care of myself it will take some time until I get tired of my new life.

Thanks to all of you for bearing with me for all those years, for all your support and friendship! I feel very fortunate that you have been part of my life. Thank you!!

There was applause all around, with smiles and nodding heads. People came up to Mom one by one to comment on her interesting life, reminisce about work projects, and wish her well in retirement. She was gracious and witty and warm.

I was mostly left alone, which suited me. I wanted to observe Mom's interactions with her coworkers. But there was nothing remiss, except perhaps the awkward thing one of her bosses said in his remarks: "Once you get to know her, you'll like her." She appeared to take it as a compliment.

After her speech I mulled over her words. Her quest for independence was about more than just supporting herself or having the freedom to do as she pleased. She wanted to recreate the place of security she was in before the war interrupted. Home ownership was a major step in that direction. After years of schooling, thirteen years of full-time employment, and the good luck to buy her house before the housing bubble, she was in a position to retire and keep living in it until it was paid off. That was nothing to sneeze at.

SIXTEEN

The Proteins

Mid-August 2019

On the Monday after the open house at Mom's, I'm on my way to work when it occurs to me we never talked with the realtor about when to reconnect. Cindy had told us we'd have a better feel for the market after the open house, and whether we could expect an offer within a week or something more like a month. While we didn't expect to hear from her last night, this morning Mom and I are on pins and needles waiting to find out how it went.

I call Cindy's office from work. The receptionist doesn't have any information and takes down my name. I put it out of my mind and spend the rest of the day so engrossed in my work that I end up leaving for home half an hour later than usual. I can't think of why this should be a problem—if I get started on dinner as soon as I get home, we can still eat within Mom's time frame. I debate calling her from the road to let her know I'm running late, then decide against it—she probably doesn't have her cell phone out and I'm halfway home already.

Leah's car is out front when I pull up; she beat me home today. I walk in the house and look around for Mom. She's in the living room sorting through one of her boxes of papers.

"Hello," I say. "I'm home."

She barely looks up. "Hello."

Now I remember what it was I forgot. "I'm sorry I'm late. I know you wanted to go to Trader Joe's. We can still go after dinner if you want."

"That's fine," she murmurs, "whatever you want." She continues shuffling papers.

Looks like everything is under control. I go into the kitchen and start pulling things out for dinner, which will be the usual salad with protein.

Leah comes in from the patio where she's been winding down with her smartphone and approaches me in the kitchen. "Oma is worried that she hasn't heard anything about how the open house went yesterday." She says this in a normal voice, but her eyebrows are raised in a way that signals it's a bigger deal than she's making it sound. "She thinks Andy might know something, but I told her probably not—the realtor has been talking mostly with you and Oma."

I nod in agreement. "If Andy knows something, he would have called us." I turn in Mom's direction and say in a louder voice, "I called Cindy's office earlier today to ask how the open house went. The receptionist left her a message to call me back, but I haven't heard anything."

"Okay," Mom says and continues sorting.

Leah comes over to survey the protein choices, of which there are a lot today. She puts in a request for leftover salmon and extra avocado on her salad. I ask her if she'd like some of the leftover sangria from last night and send her to the garage fridge to get the pitcher and pour us a couple of glasses.

Once the salads are done, Leah adds a salmon piece and dressing to hers and takes it over to the table. I ask Mom to come in the kitchen and choose a protein. Aside from the leftover pork, the others are all proteins she'll eat: salmon, precooked chicken from a package, hardboiled eggs, black beans, cottage cheese.

Mom comes in and casts a halfhearted glance at the choices. "I'll have what everyone else is having."

"We're all having something different today—it's a bunch of smaller and leftover portions. I'm having the pork, which is the oldest."

"The oldest stuff is fine with me."

"But you don't eat pork. What else do you see here that you might want?"

She turns slightly in my direction and balls her hands into fists. "I don't *know*!" she says loudly in her raspy voice, bending her body forward for emphasis. "All this time we've been eating together, you've never asked me that. Why now? What's changed?"

My muscles tense and my mind goes blank. "I didn't mean to upset you."

"I'm *not* upset!" She stamps her foot and backs away from me. "You said to eat the oldest thing, and I said fine. When have I ever complained? I just don't know what you want me to do!" She storms back to her papers in the living room.

I take slow and deep breaths, camouflaging the flush of heat and panic inside with a bland, robotic exterior. I spoon the rest of the cottage cheese onto Mom's plate and place three strips of the precooked chicken on top. I pile the pork onto mine. I bring our plates to the table where Leah is waiting quietly.

"Your dinner is ready," I say to Mom as I sit down.

Mom pauses for a moment with a folder in her hand, then stares in my direction and snaps at me. "Why are you saying that? What is it that you expect me to do?"

"Come to the table and have dinner."

She puts the folder down and comes to the table. She sits down and looks at her plate. "Can you take this meat away? I had that for lunch." I stand back up and retrieve a plastic baggie from the drawer, pick the chicken strips off her plate with it, and put them in the fridge.

We eat in silence for half a minute. "Why is everyone so quiet?" Mom demands. "You were having a fun conversation, but as soon as I come over, everyone is quiet."

Leah furrows her brow and shoots me a questioning glance. A reasonable conversation about what's going on is unlikely, but I feel compelled to at least acknowledge the tension.

I look at Mom and say, "We're not talking because of the bad mood."

"And it's all my fault. Just tell me what I'm doing wrong. I have no idea. You treat me like I'm the devil."

I resist the temptation to look at Leah. My cool robotic exterior says, "What do you mean? What did I do to make you feel I'm treating you like the devil?"

"I never said you treat me like the devil."

I'm grateful for Leah's presence—she'll be my witness to this crazy conversation.

Mom takes a bite of her salad, chews, and swallows. "Yesterday everything was fine. I felt like part of the family. Today, all of a sudden, everything is different. You don't like me at all. Leah doesn't want to talk to me." She turns to Leah. "When you came home, I tried to be nice and ask you about your day, and then you just went outside on the patio and closed the door."

Leah stares at her with disbelief. "No, Oma. I did talk to you when I first came home, just like I talked to Mom when she came home. We weren't having a *fun* conversation; it was about stuff for dinner."

"But you were talking and then when I came over it was complete silence."

"That's because I already picked out my protein. And you got upset at Mom when she asked you to choose yours."

Mom looks at the table, flustered. "I was not upset. That's just the way my voice is from the radiation treatments, and there's nothing I can do about it. I just have to live with it. I think I better go and eat in my room, so I don't bother you."

Mom gets up with her plate and leaves the table. Leah and I eat in silence, not daring to make eye contact until we hear the door close. But then we can't really talk, because my house is small and sound travels. We'll have to catch up later.

SEVENTEEN

Unhappiness

Mid-August 2019

About half an hour after Mom's outburst, I'm at the kitchen sink washing the dinner dishes. I sense someone behind me and glance over my shoulder. Mom is standing a few feet back, holding her empty plate in both hands like an offering. I step to the side and gesture at the sink with my sudsy scrubbing pad. She deposits her plate and returns to where she was standing. "Do you think we can still go to Trader Joe's?" She's perfectly calm.

"Yes, sure. I'm almost done with the dishes."

Five minutes later we're in the car and she starts talking.

"You know, I wasn't upset. It's very bad when you tell someone they're upset, because then it makes them so."

I feel an impulse to argue that she *was* upset before I said so; Leah saw it, too. My mind starts sifting through her earlier demeanor for physical details I can use to prove my case. But then I go in a different direction. "Well, it seemed like you were feeling bad about something. If you weren't upset, what would you call it then, these bad feelings?"

"I was unhappy."

"Why were you unhappy?"

"I was . . . feeling lost."

"Lost," I repeat, while in my head I work out the interpretation. Mom doesn't feel in control of things—the entire downsizing process, the seat-of-the-pants nature of the real estate business, leaving the comfort of her own home and routines for an indeterminate time, and not having a clear idea of what comes next. Perfectly understandable; those things are stressing me out, too.

Before I have a chance to say anything, she asks, "Why didn't you offer me any sangria?"

"Sangria," I repeat.

"You and Leah were having a nice conversation, and I felt excluded. Don't you know that's a trigger for me, feeling like I don't belong?"

Wow. I'm surprised at the clarity of her insight. It's true—her complaints and accusations have always been about the ways she felt rejected and neglected. The most consistent thing I did to improve our relationship after her cancer was to make sure she felt noticed and included. At the family dinner last night, I offered her small glasses of both the red and the white sangria alongside a bottle of sparkling water (her favorite drink). It didn't occur to me to offer her any tonight because it was an ordinary weeknight, and I know she limits her alcohol intake.

"I'm sorry. I didn't think you'd want any of the leftover sangria. I'll remember to offer you some next time." I knew as soon as I said the words that it wasn't about the sangria. Mom can tell I talk differently to Leah than to her. My interactions with Leah are more comfortable and easygoing. We take shortcuts in our language and understand what the other means. We don't need to explain jokes or repeat ourselves. We can sense when to move on from a topic. Mom picked up on this all last week and finally today had concrete evidence in the sangria which hadn't been offered to her.

"I know you're working so hard," she says. "I never would have gotten to this place without you."

"I want you to be happy," I say with all sincerity.

Later that evening Leah and I exchange a few texts while getting ready for bed, but the full debriefing happens the next morning over our cell phones as we commute to work. We compare notes and corroborate each other's accounts. I share that Mom feels out of place and unwelcome. Leah appreciates that I'm trying to calm things down and to help Mom feel better, but she isn't going to pretend to be okay with Mom's behavior. She offers to spend more time in her room or on the patio to decrease their interactions and the potential for conflict. I can't argue with that.

On Wednesday I take Mom to San Ramon to get some financial advice related to the sale of her house. On the way home, she starts talking about Leah.

"Does Leah say hello to you when she comes home from work?"

"Usually, but not always."

"You always say hello to me."

"That's because I know you expect it."

"Okay, that helps." She pauses for a moment. "What does Leah think of me? Of having me stay here? Does she say anything?"

"She's fine with it, although what happened Monday was stressful. She'll probably be spending more time in her room to minimize conflicts."

"Monday was stressful?" Mom seems surprised.

"Yes. At least for Leah and me."

"Oh. It's good to know I'm not the only one who feels rejected."

Now the gears in my head are going again. I had said *stressed* not *rejected*. Did Mom mean *misunderstood*? This must be the alexithymia. If only we had an emotion-translator. How different my childhood would have been. How different her *life* might have been. All the emotions Mom touched on in the last few days are part of a lifelong theme: unhappy, lost, feeling excluded and rejected. I'm understanding the connections better now than ever, but it's a different matter to bring along others who've been exposed to the worst of her off-putting behavior.

I have plans to go out in the evening. I informed Mom of this early and often. She's sitting on the couch with her papers when I tell her that her dinner salad is ready and I'm leaving.

She looks up. "Oh, *thank* you for *talking* to me. Can I *help* you with anything?"

I'm taken aback by her tone—what did I do now? Then I remember about prosody. Maybe she wants to signal to Leah who is within earshot that nothing bad will happen if you talk to her, and you may even get an offer of help. But this is not what comes across. Leah tells me later she found it extremely passive-aggressive.

"No," I tell Mom. "I don't need help with anything."

I worry all evening about leaving them alone together. They are both in bed by the time I get back.

When I wake up Thursday morning, I hear them talking with each other through my bedroom door. There is nothing alarming in their tone. By the time I come out, Leah has left for work. Mom is friendly and in a cheery mood.

"I'm not home for dinner again tonight," I remind her. "There's another salad in the fridge for you. Are you good with everything else?"

"Yes."

On Friday morning Leah catches me up over cappuccinos at the local coffee shop before we head to work. Mom has been friendly and reasonable since yesterday morning. I breathe a little easier.

At long last Andy forwards a message from Cindy. Things were slow at the open house—good traffic, but nobody left their name. We'll see if any offers come in next week. Mom and I make plans to drive to her house Sunday morning to water the ivy and collect any mail that didn't get forwarded.

On Saturday I notice a tightness in my chest—I can't seem to get a deep breath. I've had this before: it's just anxiety. Why now? Things have calmed down and we're over the hump with downsizing. But suddenly I have time to think about all the uncertainty and all the things left to do. It's overwhelming.

EIGHTEEN

The Bangladesh Trip

2009

In 2009, we were invited to a family wedding in Bangladesh, my father's homeland. The bride and I shared the same great-grandparents, which made us second cousins. The invitation came through Andy, who had made a couple of trips there and reestablished connections with that side of the family. Most of my immediate family had never visited the country.

I had other things going on, so I declined the invitation. But Leah, who was a sophomore in college, wanted to see more of the world and squeezed the trip into her semester break. Andy's then-fiancée Julie was also interested in international travel and decided to join them. Mom was pleased to be included and curious about the country she'd always refused to visit when she was married to Dad for fear of losing her right to come back home.

The four of them bought tickets on the same flight out of Los Angeles International Airport. Andy, Julie, and Leah lived in the area. Mom drove down from San Jose the day before to join Andy at Julie's place.

When Mom arrived, Andy and Julie were busy packing. Once they finished, they brought their suitcases down, then Julie went back upstairs to get her purse.

As was Mom's habit, she had brought food from her house so it wouldn't go bad. The bok choy was trimmed, rinsed, wrapped in paper towels, and put in a repeatedly rewashed resealable plastic bag. She showed it to Andy. "I brought a vegetable we can have with dinner. Or if no one wants it I can eat it myself."

"There's not enough food here for dinner. We were planning to go out to eat."

"What about my vegetables?"

"You can just leave them."

"You mean, throw them away?" Mom said, indignant.

Before Andy knew it, Mom had turned the rejection of her bok choy into a rejection of her. "You never wanted me on this trip," she said bitterly. "I don't know why I came. I'm so sorry it's too late to cancel my plane reservation."

In the meantime, Julie had come back downstairs. In their previous encounters, Mom had been sweet and engaging, leading Julie to believe Andy was exaggerating when he told her that Mom was crazy. Now Julie was shocked by the transformation.

"She was an elderly woman when I went upstairs," she later told me. "When I came down, she would not sit next to her son. She was behaving like a preschooler. I sat across from Andy and made eyebrow raises at him."

Andy wondered if he'd made a mistake inviting Mom. He'd always dealt with her outbursts by walking away until she behaved, but this time they'd be trapped together for the duration of the trip. "Of course we want you to come," he said to her with conviction. "We're all looking forward to the trip."

"Go have your dinner," Mom huffed. "I'll stay here and eat my vegetables so you can enjoy your dinner without me."

Mom went to sit in the corner of the kitchen and started eating her bok choy, raw out of the bag. Andy and Julie ordered takeout.

The next day they picked Leah up on the way to the airport. "Everyone was quiet and on edge," she told me afterwards, "but not more than typical for being around Oma."

The first leg of the trip was a thirteen-hour red-eye flight into Bangkok. When they landed, everyone was sleep-deprived and fuzzy-headed. They tried to figure out the gate of their connecting flight to Dhaka and where to get food on the way.

As Leah described it, "We were huddled in a group and speaking normally. Oma was not following along. We would say, 'Oh, we should go here,' but she didn't know what we were talking about. She would say, 'Wait, what does this mean?' and we'd have to repeat it. Exhausting! Then she would get upset that people were not telling her what was going on, even though she was standing right there with us and observing everything. The conversation was not particularly challenging, except that we were all tired. But she felt ignored, pushed aside, and purposely excluded."

Mom must have picked up on Leah's irritation because she started referring to her in the third person, calling her *my granddaughter* as if she weren't there and, in Andy's words, making everyone *so uncomfortable*—a phrase he would use repeatedly to describe Mom on this trip.

After they found a place to eat, Leah ordered a beer with her meal and tried to relax for the rest of the layover.

When they arrived in Dhaka, it was a shock to the three who had never been there before. As Julie summarized it: "Descending into Bangladesh through a brown fog. Entering the airport and noticing the most common luggage is black trash bags wrapped with duct tape. Surrounded by women draped in fabric and men with stern faces. Saved by a relative who led us outside into the mob climbing the fences enclosing the airport. Surrounded by so many people and stink. Grateful to cover face and breathe perfumed cashmere. Traffic does not move. People are everywhere. Rickshaws with skinny sweaty drivers. People and kids riding on train roofs. Families with babies and animals riding mopeds without helmets."

The relative dropped them off at the bargain hotel where Andy had booked rooms. Julie described the scene: "Hearing loogie hawking in the hallway. Boogers on the walls by our bed. Gross water, weird flusher, dirty shower. Dirty everything." There were some terrifying moments when noisy mobs ran up and down the street throwing fireballs, but thankfully it was just a Hindu holiday festival.

Aside from the pre-wedding events and festivities, there wasn't much of an itinerary. Our relatives drove them around to meetings and meals arranged on the fly with different members of the large extended family. In Julie's words, "Wonderful warm people who liked to overfeed us. Great home-cooked food." Traffic was always horrible; getting anywhere took a long time and sometimes all day, as there might be only one car available that could not hold everyone and would deliver them in batches.

In the hotel, Andy and Julie shared a room while Mom and Leah shared another. Mom wanted talking and a predictable schedule, and Leah was aggravated by the constant demands for communication and information she didn't have. "I never said anything mean," Leah reflected years later, "but she could probably tell from my body language that I wanted nothing to do with her."

At one point Andy knocked on the door of their room to go over the plan for the next day.

Leah was sitting on her bed facing the doorway. "That sounds fine," she said to him.

Mom was further inside the room. "What?" she said, looking at Leah's back. "Are you deciding for me, too?"

Leah looked over her shoulder and frowned.

"No. I was answering Andy's question."

"Oh," Mom said, her voice dripping with sarcasm. "So, it's an accident that you show me your back and leave me out of the conversation."

"That's not what I was doing," Leah said, irritated.

"Stop it, Mom," Andy chimed in. "That's not what's going on."

During breakfast at the hotel the next morning, Mom walked up to Leah, turned her back, and initiated a conversation with Andy about something irrelevant.

"Can you stop doing that?" said Leah.

"What do you mean?"

"You're trying to get back at me for last night."

"I'm just talking to Andy. Am I not allowed to do that?"

"Oh my God. Mom." Andy muttered, shaking his head.

"So, it's fine if Leah puts her back to me, but when I do it, it's not okay?"

"I didn't put my back to you to exclude you on purpose," Leah said with exasperation. "Not like you're doing right now."

"Oh, so it was an accident? How am I supposed to know that?"

Leah stood up, frustrated, and went back to their room, leaving half her breakfast. This was the first time she had tried to argue with Mom, who was either ignoring or twisting all of Leah's words into new barbs and accusations until Leah had no idea what they were arguing about. I understood this pattern so well I didn't know whether to laugh or cry when Leah described it to me.

Andy pulled Mom aside and gave her a talking-to. "Mom. You need to stop this behavior."

"And what about Leah?"

"Don't worry about Leah. She's not causing any problems."

"Oh, so it's all my fault."

"Stop. Just stop."

Mom was less inclined to argue with Andy than with the rest of us. She stuck her chin out and seethed in silence.

There was a day trip to Tangail, the village where Dad was born. They met with his only surviving sibling, a sister who was now old and frail, and saw the school that was established by their father (my grandfather). It was a moving visit. On the way back they stopped for tea with milk from a roadside stand.

The next day was the main ceremony, with wedding rituals and feasting that lasted most of the day. At different times during the festivities, each of the three women became violently ill, with projectile vomiting and diarrhea, and unable to keep anything down. Leah participated in a group dance she'd rehearsed for earlier, even though she was weak from dysentery. Julie remembered being pinned tightly into her sari and rushing back to the hotel room to get out of it before yet another purge of liquids.

Andy had the relatives drive them to a nicer hotel that had the best flushing toilets. This time Mom got a room to herself, and Leah stayed with Andy and Julie for the remainder of the trip.

"Andy said he was going to have to marry me after everything we went through on that trip," Julie said years later. "I'm grateful for these memories today. Never ever want to go there again."

Andy, the most unflappable of us, also swore "never again," but it was in reference to taking Mom on a trip.

And Mom's experience? She didn't talk about it until I brought it up a couple of weeks later. She described the events in general terms: the visit to Tangail, seeing relatives she'd met before, getting sick, the wedding.

Then she confided: "I really don't understand some people's reactions."

"What do you mean?"

"Well, Andy was . . . I don't know. But I had a lot of problems with my granddaughter. I realize I don't understand her at all."

"Oh?"

"I think after this experience, I won't try so hard to reach out to her anymore."

I nodded. This was for the best.

"I don't think anyone wanted me on this trip," Mom concluded. "I have the feeling I shouldn't have gone at all."

NINETEEN
A Week in Orange County

Mid-August 2019

Mom and I are getting ready for another visit to Southern California. Andy and Julie are going on an all-expense-paid trip to New York for a few days because Julie met her sales goals, and we'll be watching the kids while they're gone.

The timing works out well. Mom's house has been on the market for eleven days and we're still waiting for an offer. This means she has no conflicting obligations or reasons to be in the Bay Area during our trip. And we'll make excellent use of the time that the kids are in school. I've made appointments for us to tour five senior living communities in Laguna Hills and to consult with a financial advisor who specializes in helping seniors figure out options for retirement communities.

Mom and I are packing, working our way through the list of things to take. She stops when she gets to one of the items.

"What's this?" she says. "Why do we need a copy of my living trust?"

"Did you see the email from the financial advisor? That was one of the things he said to bring."

She puts on a glum face. "No, I didn't see that. Why does he need to see my trust? It has nothing to do with financial planning."

"I'm not sure what part he's interested in. Maybe the schedule of assets."

"What does he expect? That on a Sunday, I go out and find a lawyer to make the updates to the trust?"

I mentally roll my eyes. I know about the changes that need to be made, and they are minor: just new contact information for me and Mike. "No, we can bring it the way it is. It's just a consultation. We can tell him you're going to be updating it if it matters."

"I don't even know where it is. As you said, I don't have my stuff together."

I ignore this, as I haven't said any such thing. "I'm sure it's here. We took it along with all the important papers from your house."

"Does he expect me to bring the whole thing? We're going on a plane. We won't have room for it."

"It's not that big. The box I found had a bunch of drafts in it. We only have to bring a copy of the final."

"Well, I don't even know where that is. I'm so disorganized. I can't keep my stuff in order. I haven't even seen it in the ten years since I've had my two cancers."

My mind immediately goes to correct her facts: it's only been five years since she had the trust done, which was a year after her second cancer. But I keep quiet—accuracy isn't the point.

Mom continues, "As you said, I don't have it together. I'm such an idiot."

I groan inwardly. "What do you mean? When did I say that?"

"Oh, I don't know. When you were talking to someone—Andy, or your kids. I don't know."

"What was it I said?"

"I don't remember. I'm trying to forget. Something about me not knowing where my things are, not being able to keep track of important things." She pauses, then says somewhat less petulantly, "And you are right."

Good grief. "Well, why don't we see if we can find it?"

Mom's trust documents turn out to be in a stack of things I had put in her room for her to sort, along with the several boxes of papers. She's been here now for two weeks and is still working on the first box. We locate the final version of the trust among the drafts, but now that she has it in hand, she's reluctant to take it on our trip. I offer to take along the copy she gave me five years ago. This she finds agreeable, then tells me it was a really good thing we went through all this.

I'm suddenly exhausted, and in a bad mood. For the remainder of the evening, my answers to her are short and glum—"fine," "sure," "if you want," "it doesn't matter," and I'm a little heavy-handed refilling my wine as I pack the rest of my things. I wake up at 4 a.m. and can't go back to sleep. What was it she heard me say? Was I not careful enough with my words or was she just being sensitive? Most likely it was when my kids were over at her house helping sort papers, when I told them to watch for things that could be important because they were mixed in with unimportant things. Or could I have said old bills and junk mail? Does one sound worse than the other?

The following evening we're in Orange County. Andy and I review the plan for the rest of the week. Tomorrow is Tuesday, the first day of school. Andy and Julie don't have to be at the airport until later that morning, so they'll see the kids off with our help. Then I'll take them to the airport in Andy's SUV. I'll pick them up again Sunday afternoon and we'll spend a couple of hours together before Mom and I have to be back at the airport for our return trip to the Bay Area.

Mom wants to come along to see the kids off to school in the morning. They have different starting times, so we'll divide and conquer. Mom and I will take Lexie, the third grader; Andy and Julie will take the twins to kindergarten a little later. It's a twenty-minute walk to school, so Mom will make a sizable dent in the weekly steps she tracks for exercise.

It's hectic in the morning getting all the kids up, dressed, and fed. Lexie has so many supplies to bring that Mom and I each have a bag to carry as we walk her to school. We're not even halfway there when I notice Mom is falling behind.

"Oma's walking slow," Lexie complains. "I'm gonna be late."

I check the time on my cell phone. "It should be okay. We've still got time." We turn around and wait for Mom to catch up. She's walking in small rapid steps, leaning a bit to one side and focusing intently on the ground in front of her. I'm a little surprised—it didn't seem so long ago (maybe ten years?) that *I* was struggling to keep up with *her*.

"Are you doing okay?" I ask when she gets close. I can't relieve her of her bag and take off with Lexie—I'm already weighed down with the heaviest stuff. Besides, it would make Mom feel like a failure.

"Fine," she manages breathlessly without breaking her stride. We continue at a slower pace, with me sneaking glances at the time and back at Mom every couple of minutes.

By the time we find Lexie's portable and the desk with her name on it, it's a couple of minutes past the bell and most kids are already in their seats. But there's enough first-day chaos that it doesn't matter. I give Lexie a quick rub on the back and tell her I'll pick her up later from her after-school program at the YMCA.

On the walk back to the house, Mom admits it was probably too much for her. She spends the next two hours in bed recouping her strength. She doesn't offer to walk any of them to school again. In fact, she doesn't offer to help with anything else for our remaining time here.

This is a relief—it's more work for me when she helps. While she's good at chopping things for meal prep, she distracts me with questions I wish she would figure out herself: "Where can I get a spoon?" "Do you think I should use a different knife?" "Where should I put these peels?" She gets miffed if I don't immediately answer back because I'm preoccupied with something, such as running outside to flip the meat on the grill or finding the kids a snack to settle them down.

Having her help with the kids is also a mixed bag. They are loud and rambunctious, and her post-radiation voice doesn't have the volume to get their attention. In quieter moments they don't always understand what she wants, or they pretend not to understand. Then she comes to me for help. "You're so good with them," she says. "You know what to say to them and they listen."

During this trip she seems content to rest and spend time on her computer instead of imposing on me to find ways for her to feel useful and appreciated. Good. This conserves our energy for making the important decisions ahead.

TWENTY

Parenting 101

2013 - 2018

Since Mom's thyroid cancer six years ago, we've been making regular trips to Southern California to visit Andy and his family. Watching Mom with Andy's kids has sharpened my fuzzy memories of my childhood interactions with her and provided me with additional data to analyze.

Andy's family lives in Ladera Ranch, a planned community of family-friendly neighborhoods interconnected by meandering landscaped pathways and small curvy streets. One time, the kids wanted to ride bikes to a nearby park. Six-year-old Lexie was much faster than her three-year-old siblings, so we decided to split up. Mom and I would walk next to the twins on their small bikes with the training wheels while Andy and Lexie rode ahead, and we'd reconvene at the park. Andy told us Max and Kyra needed to wait for an adult to tell them they could cross the street, then he and Lexie took off.

Mom and Max were in the lead as we approached the first small intersection. Max stopped his bike and looked both ways. No cars were coming, so he started to pedal across.

Mom grabbed at his handlebars. "No!" she shouted. "What are you doing?"

"I'm going," Max said and continued to pedal.

Mom lunged forward to get a solid grip on the handlebars and was pulled along for a few steps by the momentum. "Stop! You need to listen to me!"

Max sat on the stopped bike, his feet poised on the pedals. He looked straight ahead while Mom stared at him, nostrils flaring. "Let *go*," he implored. "I wanna cross the street."

Mom mimicked his words in an exaggerated nasally voice, drawing out the words to make extra syllables: "Let *go*-oh! I wanna cross the *stree*-eet!"

Good God. It's like they're two kids on the playground. I looked around, hoping no one was watching. As Kyra and I came even with them, I caught a glimpse of my nephew's face. His deer-in-the headlights look was like a punch to the gut that stirred up long-forgotten memories of being ridiculed the same way. No, I thought, it's *not* like two kids on the playground. It's more lopsided. The child isn't allowed to taunt the adult back.

My instinct was to defuse the tension. "Looks like it's safe to cross," I said, and we were on our way again.

Mom had been in the right: Max was breaking a rule and being disobedient. Her first attempt to correct him didn't generate results, so she bore down on him and mocked his three-year-old behavior. Compliance was the goal; hurt feelings were not on her radar.

Mom was emotionally tone deaf, not understanding the extent to which her words and tone influenced the feelings of those around her. While people with alexithymia have emotions and can act in emotional ways, they don't necessarily process the information into an understanding of feelings and emotional events.[15] Mom may have understood, intellectually, that she wasn't behaving in a *nice* way, but would have shrugged it off as something that had to be done to keep the kids in line, and would have bristled at the suggestion that there were better approaches.

Mom used emotions in an externally focused, utilitarian way to achieve her parenting objectives. She learned what worked, then amplified it: mockery, sarcasm, bizarre accusations, character attacks, playing victim. If I showed my hurt feelings, she assumed I was just trying to give her a hard time and mocked me further. The idea that I could be hurt by anything she said was a foreign concept. As far as Mom was concerned, her loving feelings for her children guaranteed she'd never hurt us—to claim otherwise was hurtful to *her*.

On the outside, Mom looked like a controlling and volatile parent who imposed her will on her

---

[15] Emma Reynolds, "What It's Like to Be Emotionally Blind," *news.com.au*, August 26, 2015. news.com.au/lifestyle/health/mind/what-its-like-to-be-emotionally-blind/news-story/1cfa69056be707467f275c613396cb62.

children without regard to their feelings. On the inside, she couldn't tell when her actions were perceived as hurtful or coercive, or that she was doing long-lasting damage to the relationship. Mom had no internal gauge of her emotional impact, no sense of remorse or inclination to apologize for hurt feelings, and no conscious reason to change her behavior.

During another visit, Mom and I stayed in the girls' room while they camped out in sleeping bags on the floor of their parents' room. One morning Mom and I were getting ready to go downstairs when Lexie came in to pick out her clothes, followed closely by her mother, Julie.

"Good morning," said Mom.

"Good morning," said Julie. "Lexie, say good morning to Oma."

Mom looked at Lexie and said in a warm sympathetic voice, "No, she doesn't *have* to." Then she squatted down until she was at eye-level with Lexie and continued. "But my feelings will be hurt if you don't. Do you want to hurt my feelings?"

I was horrified. Mom was contradicting her daughter-in-law's parenting right in front of her child and in her own house. Julie pursed her lips and squinted past Mom at something in the room. I was relieved when Lexie said good morning and Julie left the room without saying a word.

This was classic Mom: she wasn't going to tell us what to do, but we were responsible for her happiness. I described the incident to Mike. He sent me a link to a video of one of his favorite philosophers, Slavoj Žižek, who calls this parenting approach more oppressive than an authoritarian one.[16] If an authoritarian parent tells you what to do, you don't have to like it. But if the parent gives the appearance of choice when there isn't one, the psychological pressure is greater—they're not only telling you what to do but how you should feel about it.

I'd felt that kind of pressure from Mom all my life and was deeply conflicted about it. Doing the right thing, even when I wanted to, also meant pleasing my tormentor, who would see it as validation of her parenting skills. It would have been easier to obey an impersonal rule.

Complying was even harder when her wishes weren't clear.

"What would you like me to do?" I once asked Mom after listening to her go on about how her children ignored and mistreated her.

"I don't want you to do anything," she said and continued to rant at me about her unhappiness. Yet, I felt enormous pressure to do something to make her feel better. But what was I supposed to do if she wouldn't tell me what she wanted? Read her mind?

Yes, apparently. Alexithymic individuals look to others to regulate and interpret their unprocessed emotions, sometimes using provocative speech or

---

[16] Open Culture, "Slavoj Žižek Calls Political Correctness a Form of 'Modern Totalitarianism,'" April 22, 2015. openculture-.com/2015/04/slavoj-zizek-calls-political-correctness-a-form-of-modern-totalitarianism.html.

language to compel a response[17] (including, perhaps, making random accusations to probe what people are thinking). Mom hadn't even figured out that she wanted me to do something, much less what.

Mom parlayed this approach into her parenting style, which involved thrusting emotions into everything and dialing up the heat to make us do things without her having to make explicit demands. Then she could feel good about her parenting, because we had done what she wanted without making her feel strict and demanding like her mother.

Mom had long complained that her mother didn't show her much love as a child. This did not jibe with my experience of my grandmother. When I was in Oma Martha's charge, sure, I had to follow her rules and household schedule, including some peculiar prohibitions due to her religious beliefs. (Playing cards were not allowed—they were of the devil.) Oma Martha, too, could be cutting with her words and lay a good guilt trip, but she didn't expect the kind of emotional caretaking Mom did. Oma Martha's boundaries were clear, and it was possible to stay out of trouble. I felt seen and humored and cared for; I never thought of her as cruel or unloving.

Still, people often treat their grandchildren differently than they did their own children. Could Oma Martha have been as harsh as Mom claimed? I doubted it. Oma Martha was sensible and not overly emotional. And Mom had the same complaint about both of us: we didn't show her our love. I

---

[17] Jason Thompson, *Alexithymic Parenting: The Impacts on Children.* (Glendale: Soul Books, 2012).

identified with Oma Martha. Mom was the one who perceived relationships differently.

Mom prioritized demonstrativeness: words and physical gestures of affection. She declared her love for us, cooed at us, and stroked us like pets. Gestures that weren't visible and concrete, where she had to infer that something was being done for her, were likely to fall into the category of things that just happen for no particular reason;[18] this would be consistent with the externally oriented thinking style of alexithymia.[19] When Mom and I started traveling together, I expended a lot of mental energy on the emotional work of interpreting her needs and smoothing her way with people, all to good effect. But she didn't seem aware of the role I played—she just knew she enjoyed my company.

In contrast, I valued the opposite things. Warm and fuzzy words and physical gestures were worthless if they didn't translate into meaningful actions such as kindness, attention, and not twisting the knife.

The Mother's Day Card Debacle of 2011 is instructive. Back then we were still in our walking-on-eggshells phase, the tension punctured by occasional skirmishes. As a gesture of goodwill, I decided to send a card instead of just calling on Mother's Day, since I knew she liked getting them. It took extra time and effort to go to the drugstore, pick out a card, sign it, address and stamp it, and

---

[18] Charlie Huntington, "Alexithymia: Definitions, Symptoms, & Examples," Berkeley Well-Being Institute. berkeleywellbeing .com/ alexithymia.html.
[19] Susan Krauss Whitbourne, "The Most Important Personality Trait You've Never Heard Of," *Psychology Today*, August 14, 2018.

put it in the mail. I patted myself on the back and waited for my brownie points. When Mom's response came, there was no recognition of my efforts or good intentions—she'd gone ballistic over my choice of card. She was stuck there, on the wording of the card, and on the one interpretation that came to her mind: I didn't love her and I wanted her to know it. When I told her I'd sent the card to make her feel valued, she backed off immediately, becoming sunny and cheerful, as if that possibility hadn't occurred to her.

But Mom had picked up on something. I'd chosen a card with the most bland and neutral wording I could find: "Wishing you the Mother's Day you deserve." I had a visceral reaction to most of the others, which were flowery and treacly and just what Mom would have loved. I couldn't get myself to buy one of those. I was resisting a lifetime of Mom's psychological pressure to provide her with a *show* of love. While I was willing to go through the motions and be polite and even friendly to Mom, I drew the line at expressing sentiments I didn't feel.

Back in 2011, my feelings told me I was at war with Mom. She was not a safe person, because she used emotions as a weapon to control people. In buying the card, I was focused on my efforts to overlook my feelings and do something nice for Mom—not a show of love, exactly, but a show of good intentions. But Mom was focused on the card and its ambiguous message, correctly reading into it my lack of affection.

During a visit to Andy's family in December 2017, we decided to eat at California Pizza Kitchen. While we waited for a table, we went outside so the kids could run around and get some of their energy out; soon we'd be inside, and they'd be expected to sit still and behave. Mom turned to me and said, "I don't remember you guys being so wild and aggressive. You never gave me any trouble."

"Hm," I said noncommittally. Of course we hadn't. She'd trained us by scolding and shaming us into acting like little adults when we were in public—kids that were loud and rambunctious were an affront, regardless of the circumstances.

On another day, Mom sat in the living room and provided a running commentary on *Boss Baby*, a new movie the kids were watching on Nickelodeon.

"What is that guy doing? He's being so mean to the other guys."

"Oh, no! They're slapping each other. That's awful!"

"Why are they all yelling?"

"This is not a good show."

Eventually Andy picked up the remote and flipped through the channels in search of something less controversial.

"Yes!" Mom said when *The Care Bears Movie* came up. "This one is much better." Kyra stayed watching with Mom on the couch while the other two left to do something else.

Mom complained to me later about the cartoons. "I don't remember them being so loud and violent when you guys were little."

"Maybe so." I nodded.

"And Andy's encouraging this kind of violence with his kids. Did you see he told Max to hit him?"

"They were practicing Jiu Jitsu moves. Max stopped when Andy said 'enough.'"

"I don't understand what happened to Andy," Mom said. "He used to be such a sweet little kid."

Mom had a rigidity about her when it came to kids' behavior. If we crossed a line, knowingly or not, her disapproval felt absolute—unmodulated by competing thoughts that we were generally good kids and weren't purposely out to get her, and impervious to alternate explanations. There was no gray area, no benefit of the doubt.

Black-and-white thinking reduces the complexity of ambiguous situations and is a feature of both autism[20] and alexithymia. Parents in these populations tend to be rigid about moral issues and adhering to social expectations, and they frequently misinterpret their child's normal inclinations, if in conflict with theirs, as misbehavior or belligerence.[21]

After one of our trips, Mom remarked that Lexie reminded her of herself: headstrong and independent and wanting to do things her way.

"Even the tantrums," she added, having witnessed a couple during our previous trips. "Did you know I had tantrums when I was a child?"

"No," I shook my head.

"I had tantrums every day. Even with people

---

[20] Psychological & Educational Consulting, "No Room for Gray Here – Black & White Thinking and Autism," April 27, 2018. psychedconsult.com/no-room-for-gray-here/.
[21] Thompson, *Alexithymic Parenting*.

who treated me well and who I loved, like my grandmother. When I had a tantrum, she would hold me on her lap and sing hymns. I still remember that and think of her when I hear those hymns." She became quiet for a moment. "I can understand the tantrums with my mother, but to this day I don't understand why I acted that way with my grandmother."

Mom had frequent emotional outbursts during my childhood, somewhere between daily and weekly. But what she was describing sounded like meltdowns,[22] an intense reaction to being overwhelmed by sensory stimuli or mental frustration that includes a loss of behavioral control. In contrast to tantrums, a meltdown can't be stopped by removing the audience—it's a physiological response that must run its course. During a meltdown, you might say or do things you don't mean, but you don't feel in control and aren't necessarily targeting anyone. Afterwards you feel better, even refreshed, but you might be embarrassed if people saw you lose control. You wish they'd forget about it, or at least not take it personally. You might be puzzled why they persist in wanting to talk to you about the stuff you said as if it were important.

Mom had these, too, maybe monthly. She became huffy and stompy and irrational, making looser and looser connections to my previous transgressions until I didn't recognize what she was

---

[22] Jessie Reimers, "Autistic Meltdowns in Adults," *Getafreshstart.com.au* (blog), January 30, 2017. Getafreshstart.com.au/autistic-meltdowns-adults/; RDIconnect, "What Is an Autism Meltdown?" Dec 20, 2019. rdiconnect.com/what-is-an-autism-meltdown/.

talking about. Afterwards she'd act as if nothing happened, or question why I was so sensitive about what she'd said when she didn't even mean it. Sometimes she'd act like she was forgiving me for making her say those things.

She still had occasional meltdowns after I moved out, but I hadn't seen one since her thyroid cancer in 2013. Except last week when I made her choose a protein for dinner.

Taken together, Mom's behavior with Andy's kids and the memories it brought up fit well into a framework of autism with alexithymia. I'm more confident than ever I'm on the right track.

Mom has trouble processing emotional information and putting herself in other people's shoes. She relies on both a rigid, concrete system of rules to order her social world, and on other people, especially her loved ones, to fill in the gaps and tend to her unformed expectations. If this doesn't go well, she becomes provocative, seeing this as a way to express her feelings and get her needs met, but without understanding the negative effect on others. This is how Mom ends up with more than her share of misunderstandings and sore feelings.

I'd never have guessed she had such a problem, given her accomplishments in the outside world and her self-assured social presentation. I figured if she were smart enough to achieve what she had in life, she must know what she's doing in the relationship realm, and I cut her no slack. The way she treated me felt intentionally hurtful, controlling, and manipulative, and I interpreted her innocent-sounding "who, me?" denial of such intentions as mind games.

Now I have an alternate explanation that makes me rethink these old assumptions. They seemed logical at the time, but it's possible I'd misunderstood Mom as much as she misunderstood me.[23] I might have played a role in keeping us trapped in our swamp of distrust.

Another thing I didn't expect is that spending time in the past still riles me up. I'd thought explaining and putting labels on Mom's behaviors would calm the intensity of the old memories, but I still become angry on behalf of the child-me. Perhaps my emotions are trying to tell me something.

When I take inventory of Mom's old behaviors, there's one that doesn't line up with my theory: the emotional gouging—the tongue lashings where she fixed me with her blazing eyes to see which hurtful accusation hit closest to home. What I've read about autistic meltdowns doesn't sync with that. Mom's emotional gouging was personal, invasive, and intentional, and it happened while she was in control of what she was saying. Alexithymia explains why she would have thought this no big deal, but it doesn't account for the way she went after me in the first place.

Maybe I'm making too much of it. Maybe I'm just overly sensitive. My theory is solid—I've done respectable work. This is as good as it's going to get. That little piece of anger may never go away.

---

[23] Damian Milton, "The Double Empathy Problem," National Autistic Society, March 2, 2018. autism.org.uk/advice-and-guidance/professional-practice/double-empathy.

TWENTY-ONE
My Grandmother

1914 - 2007

When Mom would vilify her mother, I dismissed it, because she vilified me in a similar way. Oma Martha didn't deserve Mom's accusations of cruelty and unloving behavior, just as I didn't. It took little to provoke Mom and make her lash out, and I imagined she would have been difficult to raise. But was I too willing to let Oma Martha off the hook? In light of my new theory, it's worth a deeper look.

Oma Martha was born to German parents in a small village, in a region of modern-day Poland that was then West Prussia[24] and under German control. The historical inhabitants in the early Middle Ages were Slavic tribes, but German colonization occurred as far back as the fourteenth century after conquest by

---

[24] Wikipedia, Wikipedia's "West Prussia" entry, Wikipedia's entry on the Province of West Prussia. en.wikipedia.org/wiki/West_Prussia.

the Teutonic Order. Germans and Poles coexisted for the next several centuries under sovereignties that shifted every so often due to wars, treaties, revolts, and crumbling monarchies. Toward the end of the eighteenth century, the area came under Prussian control. Prussia was a powerful German state that had come to prominence for its military victories in multiple territorial wars in Central Europe. The Prussian king Frederick the Great welcomed immigrants of diverse backgrounds to settle and farm the sparsely populated land, but he favored Germans and offered them economic incentives, while he disenfranchised Poles whom he saw as culturally inferior. By the time Oma Martha came along, Germanization had been going on for the better part of a century; the proportion of Germans in West Prussia had increased from 46 percent in 1819 to about 60 percent in 1910.

Oma Martha was the youngest of five, born in 1914 just months before the start of World War I. The fighting ended four years later with Germany's surrender. The Versailles Treaty, signed in June 1919, ceded much of West Prussia to Poland, including the district where Oma Martha's family lived (Kreis Strasburg, now Brodnica). About half the German population left the ceded areas around that time, moving to other parts of the German Reich (Realm); these were mainly civil servants, professionals, and merchants from the urban areas.[25] The majority of Germans who stayed were farmers, including Oma Martha's family. They were

---

[25] Richard Blanke, *Orphans of Versailles*. Lexington: University Press of Kentucky, 1993.

independent producers whose immediate socioeconomic status was less threatened by the change in sovereignty.

The remaining Germans were once again in the minority. Many resisted assimilation into the new Polish State. This was in part because they resented having to hand over their political power to people they'd long ruled and thought of as inferior, but there was another important reason. The German government, having not been allowed to negotiate the terms of the Versailles Treaty, contested a ceded area that allowed Poland access to the sea (the Polish Corridor). The ongoing dispute gave the German minority hope that the Reich would find a way to reclaim some of the land, thus they had incentive to stay and maintain their German citizenship and cultural identity. The Polish government saw this as a threat and tilted its policies to encourage Germans to leave, through land reforms that affected farm ownership, the disenfranchising of German public schools, and Polish language requirements.

Under the old regime, Poles had been required to learn German, but not vice versa. Most Germans hadn't bothered to learn Polish and were now at a disadvantage: workers had to demonstrate proficiency in Polish to keep certain jobs and organizational leadership positions, and Polish officials started ignoring communications in German.

When Oma Martha started school, instruction was exclusively in Polish, and German children were punished for speaking German on school grounds. Back home after school, Oma Martha and her siblings sat down again with their slates to take German lessons from their father. Oma Martha became fluent in both languages and could have passed for either nationality. For a time, she taught German to younger German children in the neighborhood. This wasn't officially allowed and became more dangerous as German-Polish relations deteriorated: people were encouraged to report neighbors who engaged in such activity, and stories of beatings or imprisonment made the rounds. One day, Oma Martha felt like she was being watched and became too spooked to continue.

Oma Martha wanted to study to become a nurse. She once told Mike that if she could have been a nurse, she wouldn't have had to get married and have children. But her father became angry every time she brought it up—traditional mores dictated that marriage and motherhood were a woman's national duty. Oma Martha's father was respected in the community, and she was afraid of displeasing him. In 1934, she married a young German man from a neighboring village whom she met through the local Baptist church. He was twenty-two and she was twenty. She moved in with him and his parents, and the young couple took over managing the family farm in Tomken. His father continued to work the land alongside them, and his mother ran the household.

This worked out well at first. Oma Martha's mother-in-law had borne thirteen children and was used to being in charge around the house. Oma Martha was needed on the farm, where she was as hard-working and productive as the men. A year later Mom was born. Oma Martha left the caretaking of her new baby girl to her mother-in-law and went back to working on the farm. When Mom was two, the family sold the farm in Tomken and bought one further north in Hoch-Kelpin, a district of Danzig[26] where Germans made up 90 percent of the population and German children weren't forced to learn Polish.

Mom and her grandmother adored each other. In Mom's words:

> *My grandmother sang songs while she was doing her chores. Sometimes she took me on her lap and sang one song after another. I followed her around wherever I could, asking questions and being in the way. She would actually pay attention to me, telling me stories about her life and what she was doing. One day she told me that when she was a child, she didn't have the patience to listen to older people and wasn't really fond of them. She found it quite endearing that I could never get enough of her stories.*

Mom was just as fond of her father.

> *From the start, I was Daddy's girl . . . He did not seem bothered by the fact that his first child was a girl and not a boy. I felt he paid a lot of attention to me. When I was old enough, he read to me from the newspaper. He taught me the letters and the words, and when I started school at barely six years old, I could already read and make him proud . . . I remember quite clearly that he loved me. He*

---

[26] Wikipedia, Wikipedia's "Free City of Danzig" entry, Wikipedia's entry about the city-state in Europe during the interwar period. en.wikipedia.org/wiki/Free_City_of_Danzig.

made me feel safe and secure. I was certain that he enjoyed spending time with me.

With her mother, it was a different story.

I felt my mother never paid much attention to me . . . I wanted her to spend time with me and show me love. I begged and I cried. I said to her, "Tell me you love me, even if you don't mean it." She told me she was doing her duty.

What did Oma Martha mean by *her duty*? Was she referring to her national duty to raise her children according to Prussian values and parenting practices? The push for Germanization in the preceding century promoted the Prussian virtues of order and diligence, including a sense of duty and obedience to authority. In the Prussian Army, the virtues took the form of self-discipline and self-denial, subordination of the self to the state or king, and toughness toward oneself. With respect to child-rearing, parents were to train their children to show immediate and unquestioning obedience, breaking their will through physical punishment or psychological manipulation if necessary, and toughening them up by denying them affection and punishing emotional expression.[27] Based on Oma Martha's description of her father as harsh, controlling, and physically abusive, this was likely the pattern in the family for generations back.

---

[27] Anne Kratzer, "Harsh Nazi Parenting Guidelines May Still Affect German Children of Today," *Scientific American*, January 4, 2019; Wikipedia, Wikipedia's "Poisonous Pedagogy" entry, Wikipedia's entry on child-raising methods considered as "poisonous pedagogy." en.wikipedia.org/wiki/Poisonous_pedagogy.

Oma Martha's parents-in-law, on the other hand, had only lived in the area since about 1902, having moved there from Zhytomyr, Ukraine. In addition to Zhytomyr, that side of the family also had roots in Warsaw, Poland, during the preceding century. Both places were under Russian control during that time. Although both Oma Martha and her husband were ethnically German, Oma Martha's family had been steeped in Prussian dictates for multiple generations, whereas her husband's family had not. This might be why Oma Martha thought her mother-in-law was too indulgent and that Mom needed a firmer hand, a continuing point of contention between them.

In this telling, Oma Martha comes across as cold and harsh, refusing her daughter the affection she obviously needs. But there could be more to the story.

Oma Martha called Mom *schwierig* (difficult), but she never used that term to describe my uncle, her other child. Mom's being autistic could account for this, as it would have brought additional parenting challenges. Mom was painfully deliberate and idiosyncratic in the way she learned and did things. Perhaps she took too long to complete tasks, or wanted to do things her way, or resisted doing things for which she didn't see a reason. Perhaps she needed extra context or repetition or reassurance. Perhaps she became frustrated and had meltdowns when things didn't go as she thought they should. These behaviors, rooted in Mom's different perceptions, sensitivities, and processes, could have made her come across as uncooperative or purposely contrary.[28]

Oma Martha would have relied on traditional methods of discipline to extract obedience and instill values of order and efficiency. But such methods are often less effective with autistic children. The recommended strategy involves patience, flexibility, and an ongoing process of trying different approaches to manage behavior. Oma Martha's mother-in-law, having raised ten or so children (those who didn't die young), would have had a larger toolbox to work with, regardless of parenting ideology.

Affectionate behavior can vary widely among autistic individuals. While some parents are concerned with their autistic children's outward lack of affection, other parents describe their youngsters as overly affectionate: hugging, kissing, or clinging to the point of making others uncomfortable.[29] This can be understood as a desire for social interaction or emotional connection without adequate recognition of personal boundaries or social norms. Tempering such behavior in a way that the child doesn't feel rejected and unloved can be difficult, and alternate ways of showing affection should be spelled out. To Mom, the word *love* meant overtly affectionate words and gestures and not much else. Oma Martha probably noticed Mom's single-mindedness and tried to explain that she looked

---

[28] Mark Hutten, "Addressing the Root Causes of Disobedience in Kids on the Autism Spectrum," *My ASD Child* (blog), August 2017. myaspergerschild.com/2017/08/addressing-root-causes-of-disobedience.html.

[29] Tony Attwood, *The Complete Guide to Asperger's Syndrome (Autism Spectrum Disorder)*, rev. ed. (Jessica Kingsley Publishers, 2008).

after Mom in ways mothers were supposed to (doing her duty), and that this was also important. But her mother-in-law indulged Mom's desire for affection, providing a palpable contrast. Mom maintained her tunnel vision and her preference for her grandmother.

Mom claimed Oma Martha didn't teach her basic household skills. That would have been unusual: children raised on a farm were expected to contribute from an early age. Most likely Oma Martha tried but gave up when Mom didn't catch on. I see Mom's struggles first-hand when it comes to cooking a meal from scratch. I can give her a recipe for a side salad and lay out all the ingredients, and she'll come back to me repeatedly with questions about utensils and sizes and how to prepare the cooked portion and where to put the trimmings. Without my constant attention, it would take her twice as long.

Mom once told me Oma Martha still helped her get dressed years after she should have been old enough to do it herself. "I had trouble with the buttons," she admitted. Dyspraxia,[30] often seen in autistic children, involves a delay in motor skill development that can affect tasks such as buttoning clothes and tying laces, cooking (pouring, kneading, cutting, whipping) and other household chores, and a host of activities that require coordination (e.g., brushing teeth, writing, riding a bike).

There is no indication Oma Martha was physically abusive. But she had a sharp tongue, and we had anecdotal evidence she wasn't above

---

[30] Mark Hutten, "Dyspraxia in Kids on the Autism Spectrum," *My ASD Child* (blog), June 2018. myaspergerschild.com/2018/06/dyspraxia-in-kids-on-autism-spectrum.html.

calling her children stupid. (My uncle liked to tell the story of how Oma Martha had told him, "Du bist zu dumm und zu faul" ["You're too stupid and too lazy"] to go to university.) Emotional manipulation was part of Oma Martha's playbook, too. When Mom and her brother were older, Oma Martha would occasionally take to her bed, sometimes for days, after an argument with one of them. They suspected she feigned illness to get sympathy and manipulate the offender into giving in.

Oma Martha was primed by her upbringing and cultural background to prioritize obedience and order, to see nurturing as spoiling, and to punish emotional outbursts and other actions that looked like misbehavior. She could be critical, and she had a manipulative streak. But she was also raising an undiagnosed autistic child without the information and guidance we have today. And running a farm. *And* dealing with the war and its aftereffects. I'm not sure I would have done any better.

After I was born, Mom left me with Oma Martha during the work week for the first year of my life, since my parents couldn't afford childcare. Then, Mom got a better job in a different town. We moved away and Mom put me in a daycare facility nearby. Oma Martha was heartbroken. After that I saw my grandparents maybe a handful of times a year. Oma Martha hugged me tight and blinked back tears every time we said goodbye.

When Leah was three and I was expecting her twin brothers, Mom arranged for Oma Martha to come from Germany and stay with us for a few weeks. Oma Martha was happy to be involved. She flitted about, cooking and doing laundry and looking after Leah, which was difficult because they didn't speak each other's language. By the time I went into labor, they were used to each other and did fine on their own during the half day my husband and I were both away at the hospital. After the boys and I came home, Oma Martha stayed with us for another two weeks. On one of those days, I returned to the house after a solo trip to the store and found her trying to soothe one of my crying boys by rocking him in her arms and belting out a hymn at the top of her lungs.

Mom's attitude toward Oma Martha softened after Opa Herbert died in 2002 and Mom's brother told her he wanted their mother to move in with him.

"I was shocked," she told me, recounting the conversation to me years later. "I asked my brother why he would do that."

"What did he say?" I asked.

"He talked about all the things that happened in 1940, the year he was born and when I was four. That year, our father was drafted into the German Army, our grandfather died, and suddenly our mother had to run the farm all by herself."

"That sounds overwhelming."

"Yes," Mom nodded. "I knew about those things, but I never looked at the situation from her point of view before. Five years later we had to leave our home to flee the Russians. She packed up our things and had to make decisions about where we were going—without her husband, without even knowing where he was—and we became war refugees. Looking back, I can only marvel at her accomplishments and how hard she worked for us. Can you imagine what she went through?" Mom shook her head, then continued.

"The years between 1940 and early 1945 were hard for my mother. I was in school then and I caught one childhood disease after another. My brother also got sick with a couple of them. My mother made it a point to take care of her sick children herself, on top of all the hassle with the farm. She was the one who kept track of my symptoms, consulted with the doctor, put cold compresses on my forehead for my fever, and fed me chicken soup."

"She took good care of you," I said.

Mom nodded. "When I was a child, I didn't have it in me to comprehend what she had to deal with. I gave my mother a hard time. I didn't listen to her, and I was disobedient."

I nodded, amazed at Mom's contrition, and we left it at that.

Oma Martha's last visit to the Bay Area was in 2004, just after she'd turned ninety. When I saw her together with Mom, I sensed something was different. The tension between them was gone. They hugged and kissed and addressed each other with affectionate nicknames.

But my relationship with Mom was still contentious back then. When Oma Martha was alone in the car with Mike and me, after having witnessed our strained interactions with Mom, she uncharacteristically broke down.

"Lass sie nicht allein," ("Don't leave her alone,") she implored, sobbing.

"Man kann nicht mit ihr reden!" ("She's impossible to talk to!") I complained.

"Sie war immer schwierig." ("She was always difficult.")

I was quiet after that, but Oma Martha's words weighed on me.

Later that year, Oma Martha moved in with my uncle and aunt who lived in Sweden. I visited them with my family three years later, after Oma Martha had suffered a series of strokes and developed dementia. She was happy to see us, even if she couldn't keep track of who we were. She mistook Leah and me for each other and for Mom, who wasn't even there. She was confused about who was staying where—at one point she tried to leave after we said our goodbyes, thinking she was the one who was visiting. At the end of our last day together, everyone held hands in a circle in the living room while Oma Martha said a rambling twenty-minute prayer of gratitude and appeals for our guidance and protection. Not two months later, she was gone.

TWENTY-TWO

Unmasking

Late August 2019

Mom and I tour five senior living communities in Laguna Hills during our babysitting week at Andy's. The month-to-month cost for a one-bedroom apartment is pricey, but she'll get three meals a day and weekly cleaning. "Like being on a cruise," says one of the sales representatives. We visit the financial advisor who confirms that, after the anticipated proceeds from her house, Mom is in no danger of running out of money with any of the options.

Mom's charm is on display as we chat with the sales staff at each place. She's social and cheerful and says things with just the right level of humor and self-deprecation to win people over. When asked what activities she likes, she says with a mischievous twinkle in her eye, "Oh, you know, old people like me won't be getting into too much trouble." Everyone smiles. At another place, one of the reps takes me aside and says, "Your mom is so cute."

Occasionally Mom's tone is different. We're in one of the dining halls enjoying the complimentary lunch with our guide from the senior placement center when the wait staff takes too long to bring Mom's decaf coffee at the end of the meal. "They've forgotten about me—I'm just an old woman," she grouses with enough rancor that I see our guide give a start.

I've read enough by now to understand that Mom's talent at interacting with people—the charm and social skills that once made me doubt she had autism—comes from autistic masking. This refers to deliberately studying and copying the behavior of others to camouflage autistic traits and fit in.[31] I've always envied Mom her social skills, but I hadn't realized they don't come naturally: they've been honed painstakingly over many years. A common approach is to copy the intonations and mannerisms of actors on TV shows. Mom liked to watch soap operas when she was younger, which may be why her tone is often tinged with melodrama. She might sound overly cheerful, excessively polite, winkingly droll, haughtily self-righteous, bitterly sarcastic.

Autistic masking takes mental effort. When it's not needed or the person is under stress, the mask drops, revealing markedly different behavior. During a trip to Southern California in 2015, our

---

[31] L. Hull et al., "Development and Validation of the Camouflaging Autistic Traits Questionnaire (CAT-Q)," *Journal of Autism and Developmental Disorders* 49, no. 3 (2019): 819–833.

family decided to have dinner at a popular restaurant in Culver City.

It was loud and busy. There were seven of us, and we waited over half an hour for a booth. When they seated us, everyone piled in before Mom so she'd get an aisle seat and wouldn't have to slide along the bench. After we had a moment to look at the menu, the waiter came to greet us and see if we were ready to order. He stood next to Mom and talked loudly across the table so all could hear. Mom twisted around and stared up at him.

"Are you talking to me?" she accosted him.

He turned his head to look at her. "I was talking to everyone."

"And not to me?" Mom said sternly, offended.

He hesitated, and I jumped in with Mom's order: "She'll have the salad with salmon."

He took the remaining orders, and the rest of the evening passed without incident. I dropped Mom off at our motel room after dinner because she was tired, and then I rejoined the others at Leah's apartment where we dissected Mom's present and past social transgressions.

"Why did she say that to the waiter? Did she not understand he was talking to all of us?"

"Yeah—why would he come over and just talk to her? That doesn't make sense."

"She always needs extra attention."

"It's stressful going places with her."

Mom was a capable, charming, put-together person who disrupted the flow of things because she wanted attention. I viscerally understood this way of interpreting the situation—it was like a comfortable old blanket. But my views had shifted since her thyroid cancer, and I volleyed an alternative narrative into the conversation:

"I think she processes information differently."

"How would that explain what she said to the waiter?"

I wasn't sure about that.

Looking back, it could have been an auditory processing issue,[32] common in people with autism. Mom couldn't isolate the waiter's voice through the din. She was out of her comfort zone and too stressed to keep her mask up and say things in socially appropriate ways. Or she thought the waiter wasn't someone she needed to mask for—it wouldn't be the first time we'd seen Mom be rude to wait staff.

The post-restaurant gabfest was illuminating. Mom and I were getting along better by then—I was somewhat protective of her, and I intervened on her behalf with the waiter. Yet I felt a perverse satisfaction in hearing others dish about her behavior. A holdover, it seems, from the days before the cancer.

Back then, I would not have intervened with the waiter. My habit was to let Mom flounder when she made a misstep. I told myself she was a grown-up and didn't need any help, but perhaps it was also my way of paying her back for fooling the world into thinking she was such a sweet and loving person. I

---

[32] Fahimeh Mamashli et al., "Auditory Processing in Noise Is Associated with Complex Patterns of Disrupted Functional Connectivity in Autism Spectrum Disorder," *Autism Research* 10, no. 4 (2017): 631–647.

harbored a healthy dose of animosity toward Mom. Why wouldn't I when she felt the same about me? She was not someone who gave me the benefit of the doubt. Throughout my life, if things were ambiguous in a conflict, she ferreted out the explanation that put me in the worst light and then harangued me about it, treating my protestations as attempts to trick her. Her insistence on seeing me as bad and deceitful in these situations burned through my trust and goodwill faster than she could replenish them when she was in an effusive mood—my net balance with Mom was always in the red.

It will be a few years after our downsizing project before I'll come to understand the source of this dynamic. A story will pop into my newsfeed about an autistic woman initially misdiagnosed with borderline personality disorder (BPD). I'll scroll past it, figuring I already know what's going on with Mom. But the topic will percolate in my head, and several days later I'll read the article and follow one of the links to the website of Dr. Megan Neff, a psychologist diagnosed with autism and ADHD late in life.

Dr. Neff explains that BPD and autism have overlapping traits and can look very similar but are distinct conditions with different underlying causes.[33] Scanning through the side-by-side comparison, I'll realize with a shock that Mom's old behaviors that I

---

[33] M. A. Neff, "BPD vs Autism," *Neurodivergent Insights*. Neurodivergent insights.com/misdiagnosis-monday/boderline-personality-disorder-or-autism.

found so distressing are aligned more with BPD than with autism: her fears and emotional upsets reflect relationship conflicts rather than sensory or cognitive frustration.

Interestingly, people can have both conditions, a possibility I hadn't considered before. In my initial investigation decades ago, I'd rejected both autism and the cluster B personality disorders because neither sufficiently accounted for Mom's behavior. Mom had the emotional reactivity and mood swings of BPD but seemed too stable in other aspects of her life. She had the unusual thinking patterns and theory of mind issues of autism, but this didn't account for her deeply personal attacks and emotional gouging. When I tackled the puzzle again during Mom's downsizing, I started from a clean slate and came up with only autism and alexithymia, because those were the behaviors I was seeing. But this new piece of information will remind me how strongly BPD resonated with me when I first discovered it, and I'll start a new search to refresh my mind and find updated information.

BPD is associated with a pattern of intense emotions, unstable relationships, a poor sense of identity, and impulsivity. A couple of criteria described in the DSM[34] sound like the authors were in my childhood home witnessing what was going on. Criterion 2: Individuals with BPD cycle between extremes of idealization and devaluation in relationships, with no gray area. In the idealization

---

[34] American Psychiatric Association, *Diagnostic and Statistical Manual of Mental Disorders*, 5th ed. (Washington, DC: American Psychiatric Association, 2013).

phase, the other person is seen as perfect and wonderful, and the individual with BPD may be nurturing and empathetic. But this can change quickly if the person is perceived to not care enough or fails to *be there* on demand, leading the individual with BPD to view them as *cruelly punitive*. Criterion 8: Individuals with BPD "frequently express inappropriate, intense anger or have difficulty controlling their anger. They may display extreme sarcasm, enduring bitterness, or verbal outbursts. The anger is often elicited when a caregiver or lover is seen as neglectful, withholding, uncaring, or abandoning."

A few other references are also eerily accurate. Individuals with BPD: (1) are hypersensitive to rejection and tend to interpret neutral incidents as negative,[35] (2) provoke others with "wild accusations and exaggerations . . . , illogical statements, absurd arguments . . . , escalating hostility for no apparent reason . . . ,"[36] and (3) skewer people with their eyes in attempts to gain attention or control.[37]

At that point I'll have read enough. These

---

[35] Roberta Bortolla et al., "Negative Bias and Reduced Visual Information Processing of Socio-emotional Context in Borderline Personality Disorder: A Support for the Hypersensitivity Hypothesis," *Journal of Behavior Therapy and Experimental Psychiatry* 69, 101589 (December 2020), doi.org/10.1016/j.jbtep.2020.101589.

[36] David M. Allen, "Responding to 'Borderline' Provocations – Part III," *Psychology Today* (blog), January 27, 2014. psychologytoday.com/us/blog/a-matter-of-personality/201401/responding-to-borderline-provocations-part-iii.

[37] Grouport, "The Connection Between Borderline Personality Disorder and the Stare," grouporttherapy.com/blog/borderline-personality-disorder stare.

behaviors hadn't caused enough problems in Mom's life to garner a clinical diagnosis of BPD, but they featured prominently in our old relationship problems. And did those traits just disappear? Decades ago BPD was considered extremely difficult to treat and unlikely to improve over time, but updated evidence points to the effectiveness of therapy and a receding of BPD symptoms with age.[38]

Mom had done a lot of work on herself—over ten years of therapy, purportedly for depression. She became better at talking about feelings, emotions, and relationships, even though what she said didn't always make sense (e.g., our Rational Discussion). She'd drop an occasional insight or concession: "I was not a perfect mother." "Don't mind me—I'm just a childish old woman." "You're not the same as me. You think differently and you come to different conclusions about things. I have the feeling somehow that I don't know you at all." It wasn't enough to earn my trust at first—she still sniped at me for the same old reasons, albeit more eloquently (e.g., the Mother's Day Card Debacle). These incidents decreased dramatically after her thyroid cancer, but Mom's BPD symptoms didn't disappear entirely. She still has rejection sensitivity and blips of lashing out: the accusation that Mike didn't want to be around her, the pre-emptive self-directed sarcasm when she wasn't getting enough done, the meltdown over the sangria.

It's straightforward to fill in the remaining gaps. Mom is autistic, and "an Autistic neurotype makes

---

[38] *DSM-5*

a person more vulnerable to developing BPD,"[39] especially in an invalidating environment.[40] WWII was devastating for Mom. She lost the two people she loved most by the age of seven—her father to Stalingrad in the east, and her grandmother to Gelsenkirchen in the west, where Oma Martha sent her to live with relatives as the Eastern Front encroached (and her age and contentiousness were making her a liability). After that, Mom was raised in an environment that taught children their war traumas were nothing to complain about. This attitude, grounded in Prussian reverence for toughness and bearing suffering silently, persisted in many German communities for years after the war, including in the school system.[41] These *war children* grew up and led outwardly productive lives, but tended to have mysterious health and relationship problems that could be linked to their repressed emotions, including symptoms later identified as PTSD (post-traumatic stress disorder).

Mom's BPD traits were in full bloom by the time she became a mother, and protecting myself against them was my primary focus. Whatever autistic behavior might have been in the background, I barely noticed. During normal development, children learn to reconcile their good and bad experiences of someone into a whole, if imperfect,

---

[39] Neff, "BPD vs Autism."
[40] Kristalyn Salters-Pedneault, "Emotional Invalidation During Childhood May Cause BPD," Verywell Mind, updated February 20, 2021. verywellmind.com/emotional-invalidation-425156
[41] Wikipedia, Wikipedia's "German childhood in World War II" entry, Wikipedia's entry on how the Second World War impacted the life of children born in that era (*war children*). en.wikipedia.org/wiki/German_childhood_in_World_War_II.

person. I was able to do this with other people, but not with Mom—her good and bad parts were too far apart. I chose the hostile version as my internal representation of her. It was safer that way, because then she wouldn't catch me off guard.

    I'll make a final adjustment to my theory: Mom is autistic with alexithymia, and has BPD traits that developed from early relationship trauma and receded with age, therapy, and her brush with death from thyroid cancer. The child-me will feel seen, and the remnant of my anger will dissipate.

TWENTY-THREE
The Offer

Late August 2019

On the Friday of our babysitting week at Andy and Julie's house, we tour the fifth and final senior living facility. Mom's interactions with the sales staff divert her attention from details she should be focusing on. As we walk down the hallway to view a model apartment, she talks about fitness with the tour guide and mentions the Sierra Club. The young man has never heard of the Sierra Club, so Mom proceeds to educate him. He opens the door to the one-bedroom unit, and we file in. As the rest of us look around, her attention is on him as she continues talking about camping, hikes, mountains, and the locations she's been to with the Sierra Club.

"This kitchen is just the right size for you," I interject during a brief pause in her monologue.

Her eyes flit back to the young man as if I hadn't said anything. "You can meet people there that have the same interest in nature." She follows us out without even looking at the bathroom. Later she'll remember nothing about the layout and will rely on me to tell her if she liked it. I guess that's okay—I should know by now what she likes.

In the end we settle on a favorite: Evergreen Meadows with their roomier layouts and a Trader Joe's within walking distance. They have many apartment units, and one becomes available every month on average. We'll start the application process when we have firmer timing on the sale of the house.

That same Friday we get an offer on the house. By the time I open the email to look at the offer, Andy who is on New York time has already reviewed it and had a brief chat with Cindy. He says it's a good offer and Mom should take it. I read through all fifteen pages while Mom is lying down for her post-lunch rest. The potential buyers are offering Mom's asking price, but the offer is contingent on the sale of their condo. Cindy would be the agent for both Mom and the buyers, something called dual representation. This is allowed as long as it's disclosed. Everything looks to be in order. I feel a mix of excitement and hope.

That afternoon Mom and I sit at the dining table with my phone on speaker and we have a conference call with Cindy. She tells us about the buyers. They're an Indian couple with a two-year-old son; the man works in the tech industry. The house is a great fit for their family, including a front door that faces the right direction, and the move has been blessed by their respective parents back in India. Cindy repeats the key points of the offer and what a good opportunity this is, and that she'd be overseeing both ends of the transaction so communication should go smoothly. Mom has no objections to anything she's heard. "You and Andy both looked at the offer and agree it's a good one," she says, looking at me. I confirm. She agrees to go through all the information and DocuSign her acceptance by tomorrow morning.

Before ending the call, Cindy mentions she wants to go ahead with the second open house planned for this weekend—it wouldn't hurt to generate more options if this offer falls through. I don't remember hearing about a second open house, but it shouldn't be a problem—we won't even be back in the Bay Area until Sunday evening. Mom doesn't say anything, so I tell Cindy it sounds fine.

After I pick up the kids and deal with dinner, Mom and I talk about the offer. Because it's contingent on the sale of the buyers' condo, we don't have an exact closing date on Mom's house. There's a cascade of events that needs to happen first. The buyers will put their condo on the market no later than five days from now. They'll have seventeen days after that to get an offer and go into escrow on their condo, which will trigger thirty days of escrow on Mom's house. I sketch out the range of dates and make sure Mom understands that the timing won't be firmed up until the buyers get an offer on their condo and that Cindy wants to keep showing the house during that time. This means Mom will continue to stay with me for another one to three weeks.

Mom's eyelids look heavy, and she isn't saying

much. She wants to take care of the documentation tonight, so she doesn't lose sleep about having to do it in the morning. She turns on her computer and finds the email with the DocuSign link, and I talk her through opening the document for review. She starts scrolling from one signature to the next.

"Don't you want to read what you're signing?" I ask.

"No, I just want to get it done. You and Andy both read it, right?"

I assure her again that we did, and she finishes and goes to bed. I allow myself a glimmer of elation. I know she didn't absorb all the details, but I'm delighted we didn't need to stay up and debate minutiae. She signed a contract with a conditional timeline, and we found a place for her to move. This was a good week.

But there's no rest for the weary. On Saturday I supervise the kids while Mom pesters me with one technology issue after another as if I'm her own personal IT technician. "Where's the folder we created to save the real estate documents? I can't find it." Of course we can't—it's Windows 10. And the DocuSign links have expired so she can't regenerate copies. Then, "Can you help me sync my Fitbit?" I don't have a Fitbit and know next to nothing about syncing one, but something I did at my house a couple of weeks ago worked, so now she wants me to do it again. In the meantime, she has intermittent computer issues that rebooting doesn't entirely fix, like blank screens, 100 percent CPU usage, and a Windows C++ runtime error. "I don't know what's going on with your computer," I tell her and count my blessings this didn't start last night while she was DocuSigning. Finally, she gives up and puts her computer away.

I've just gone upstairs to check on the kids when I hear her call me. "Where did you go?" she says after I come back downstairs to see what she wants. "Look, my phone doesn't have Wi-Fi. Do you know the password?" The blood rushes to my head, and I feel a flash of panic and nausea. The Wi-Fi password used to be stuck on the fridge with a magnet, but Andy logged me in several visits back with a new one that wasn't displayed in the open. He had logged in Mom's computer, too, but apparently not her phone. I slog upstairs and scan the bulletin boards and the tops of their desks for any scrap of paper with letters and numbers but find nothing. Would Andy be able to tell me where it was if I called him? I envision a wild goose chase as he directs me to look in one place after another. It's all too much work. Back downstairs I look over every inch of the fridge, repeating the phrase, "I don't know," until Mom says, "Let's let it be for now."

Later that night Lexie and I are looking for Bella the cat, wanting to make sure she didn't sneak out the front door while the kids were going in and out to play. Mom is in the kitchen preparing her oatmeal for tomorrow when Lexie walks past and into the garage.

"Do you see Bella?" I call to Lexie in the garage.

Mom looks over at me with a confused frown and says, "What?"

"I'm talking to Lexie."

"What?"

"Lexie. I'm talking to Lexie."

Mom looks perplexed, then sees Lexie come back in from the garage. "Oh, you were talking to Lexie. I didn't see her."

Mom covers her oatmeal to soak for the night and says without looking at me, "You know, I didn't even see Lexie. Am I supposed to know you were talking to her? And here I am, just a thing."

My skin prickles all over. *Oh, God. Please let this be over soon.*

TWENTY-FOUR
Missing Pieces

Late August 2019

There is danger in assuming Mom has absorbed all the necessary details. Once we're back in the Bay Area, I make a printout of the offer on her house and highlight the sections related to timing. I leave it with her to review and get started on dinner.

I'm sautéing onions when she comes into the kitchen with the printout. "What's this?" she says, pointing. "It says here the house has to be vacated five days before close of escrow. Why are they kicking me out before escrow is closed?"

"It's probably a cushion to make sure all the last-minute stuff gets done."

"Does that mean they're giving me the money five days earlier?"

"No, that's not how it works."

"Well, they can't do that. That's not right."

"I think it's standard for California real estate contracts. The offer is on a standard template."

"I've never heard of such a thing," she says as I chop the bell peppers.

"Well, you've never sold a house before."

"Yes, I have."

"Oh, that's right. The pink house, after your divorce in 1976. And there wasn't anything like that?"

"No, it was much simpler."

"Well, I have no idea what the real estate laws were back then, but I have the contract from when we sold our house a couple of years ago. I can get it after dinner, and we can verify."

There are a few moments of quiet. Then she starts again.

"Who's paying the bills for those five days? Will the buyers get to move in during that time?"

"No, they can't move in until after escrow closes."

"Well then why do I have to move out? They can't do that."

She hounds me as I prepare our separate meals—one with pork, sautéed vegetables and white rice for Leah and me, and the usual salad for her—and I'm having trouble focusing. Do I need to worry she'll blow things up? I decide to draw her attention away from the realtor and the real estate system.

"You can blame Andy and me," I say, "we both read the offer."

"Then why didn't you tell me that was in there? You made me do the DocuSign thing and press all those buttons without even reading it."

"That's not true. I said you should read those sections you were DocuSigning."

"It was late and I was tired. It was dark and the print was too small. What was I supposed to do?"

"The five-day thing is standard—Andy and I didn't think to make a point of it. It should be okay. We can plan for it."

"Well, I should have had a choice about that. Where am I supposed to live for those five days, in a hotel?"

"No, you come back here to my house. That's better than a hotel, right?"

"Well yes, of course it's better. That's not the point. It's the principle. Why does it have to be five days? That's not right."

"Your salad is ready. Why don't you go ahead and eat? Leah's and my food won't be ready for another fifteen minutes."

"I will do that. It looks so delicious."

After dinner I find the offer on the house we sold a couple of years ago. It has the same requirement to vacate five days before close of escrow. I show it to Mom. "Looks like it's standard."

"Well, how should I know that? I've never sold a house before."

Later that night I have a flashback to the late '80s. Mom had lived in her rent-subsidized house for ten years when the owners needed to sell it because they were getting a divorce. Mom refused to move out. Her reasoning was she'd been living there so long and was a good tenant, so she deserved to stay and not be kicked out. It wasn't until she was threatened with losing the Section 8 benefit that she went looking for another place to live. I had moved out three years earlier but came back to help pack.

While I was there, the new owner came by and harassed her for still being on the property—she was supposed to have been out a month ago. Clearly Mom had not taken to heart *that* deadline.

I bring up the subject again the next day. "That thing about having to vacate five days before close of escrow, that's a standard part of the California real estate contract," I repeat over dinner.

"Well," she says, picking up where we left off, "I'm still paying the bills during those five days. And I'm not allowed to live there? Who's benefiting from that?"

"The extra days are probably to ensure enough time to get everything done. Things always take longer than expected. If we need more time in the house and everything else is going smoothly, I'm sure the buyers won't object if we go a day or two into the five days."

"They think I'm just a feeble old woman who can't get things done."

"It has nothing to do with you personally. It's part of the standard California real estate contract."

"It's not fair."

"Then it's not fair for all the people in California who sell their houses."

"That's right."

"Well, you can ask Andy about the five days and see if there's anything to be done about it—he's the one with the real estate license."

"Oh, I'm not going to bring it up with Andy."

"No?"

"No. I'll just talk to you about it."

Well. I shouldn't be surprised. Andy would have

shut her down after a few minutes, saying something firm and definitive like, "Mom, that's just the way it is." But I engaged with her for nearly an hour between today and yesterday, rehashing the same points over and over to make them stick, while she was never planning to revolt in the first place. I've been subjecting myself to verbal sparring with Mom, and for what? So she can shift her stress to me, like she always does? I clench my jaw and take a breath. I'm a sap. I've been enabling her bad behavior with nothing to show for it.

Some weeks later the topic comes up again. Mom makes a small flurry of protest about moving out five days before the closing date, then tells me, "Thank you for going through all this stuff with me—it's really helpful."

Then it occurs to me: this is how Mom processes information that's unfamiliar or anxiety-provoking, even if she's already made a decision about it. It's called perseveration[42]—she wasn't intending to be difficult. I reflect on the exhausting back-and-forth when she challenged me about getting the pod. What was it she had said? "I'm not arguing, only trying to understand."

The weekend after we get back from Orange County, we drive to Mom's house to water the plants, collect the mail, and make sure everything's in good shape.

I come inside after watering the ivy. Mom is sweeping. She remarks on how much dust there is.

---

[42] "Perseveration," *Fandom Autism Wiki*. autism-advocacy.fandom.com/wiki/Perseveration.

"It must be because the door to the laundry room was left open. There's a vent to the outside and it lets a lot of dust in."

"It could also be from the open house last weekend."

She stops sweeping. "What open house?"

I feel a pang of guilt. "Cindy said she was going to hold another open house here last weekend."

"Why didn't I know about this?"

"She told us at the end of the phone call at Andy and Julie's, the one where we discussed the offer on the house." Silence. "You were there during that conversation. Cindy was on speakerphone, remember? At Andy and Julie's."

She starts sweeping again, shaking her head. "There must be something really wrong with me that I didn't get that information." I look at her, not certain what to say next.

She speaks again, now with a snippy edge to her voice, a mix of wounded and haughty. "I better just get used to being invisible. That's what I need to do. Stay out of the way and not bother anyone."

I should know by now this isn't about me. She's communicating her frustration and hoping I'll say something to make her feel better. But it still feels like coercion, and I can't get myself to respond in a supportive way. I fall back on the question I asked after she flung sarcastic barbs at me in Weekend 8. "Are you upset?"

She switches to a sincere tone. "No, no, I'm not upset."

"I'm sorry you don't feel I'm giving you enough information."

"No, it's not you. You're nearly perfect, and you're working so hard. I know you're focusing on the important things. If you miss something here or there, that's okay. Nobody's perfect."

Well. It worked again—to ask about her feelings instead of assuming I knew what they were. But once more I don't know what to say next. I nod without looking at her, not knowing if she sees me, and the conversation is over. We don't talk about why Mom didn't catch what Cindy said at the end of the conference call. We don't talk about Mom's lifelong pattern of missing important pieces of spoken information and then blaming others for excluding her. We're still a long way from having that kind of conversation.

Later as we get into the car to go home, she's in a contemplative mood. "Do you think I'm satisfied with what I've accomplished in my life?"

"I hope so."

"I do, too."

TWENTY-FIVE
Unlocking Doors

Early September 2019

Within a week of Mom accepting the offer on her house, the buyers' condo is on the market.

We're once again in the position of waiting every day for a call, but now there's a time limit of two weeks—the buyers will lower the asking price on their condo if necessary. Otherwise, Mom can back out of the contract and look for a new buyer. Nobody wants that.

The days at my house pass relatively incident-free, although there are odd conversations about grapes, a broken garbage disposal, and shenanigans with locking doors.

One night after dinner Mom gathers her usual after-dinner fruit while I get out some slices of zucchini bread.

"What's that?" she says.

"Zucchini bread. Leah brought it home from work. A coworker made it."

Mom looks at Leah. "Do you have one coworker?"

Leah looks puzzled. "Not just one. I have many coworkers. This coworker is always looking for ways to use up the excess zucchini in his garden."

"Oh yeah?" Mom finishes eating her cut-up pieces of melon, then gestures at her moon grapes. "Do you not like my grapes?"

I'm not sure if she wants me to admire them or if she's offering to share. "I don't eat grapes that often," I tell her to convey I'm not interested.

Leah is more direct: "I don't feel like having any right now, but thank you."

After a moment Mom says, "Have you ever seen grapes like these?"

"Yes," I tell her, "I've seen them at Costco."

"Aren't they interesting?"

Leah and I agree. We google the unusual elongated grapes on our phones and read out the information, none of which I retain for more than a minute.

One day I come home from work to find bright green crumbly bits blanketing the bottom of the left kitchen sink—the garbage disposal finally gave out as Mom fed it some decomposing broccoli. She's apologetic and spends fifteen minutes describing in detail how something was wrong with the broccoli (did someone squish it?), that it took her over an hour to trim away the bad parts, and that she didn't eat lunch until two. She's saved the bad pieces in a baggie to show me, as well as the parts she cooked and the cleaned trimmed parts she intends to cook tomorrow.

We continue with mutual apologies: me for not checking the prepackaged broccoli more closely when I bought it two days ago and Mom for leaving a mess and not getting to the dishes on the other side of the sink. I assure her all is good—the garbage disposal needed to be fixed anyway.

Mom does have a habit of conveying excess information. Leah works from home one morning and describes to me later how Mom kept interrupting her with updates on her activities.

"I'm going to do my steps now. In the living room."

"I'm going for a walk now. I'll be back later and I have a key, so don't worry."

"I'm done with my oatmeal."

"Are you done in the bathroom? I'm going to wash my body now."

"Do you know what's under this bowl?" Mom picks up the upside-down bowl to reveal a pile of peeled pistachios on a saucer; the bowl is to keep them safe from the cat. "I opened these nuts, and nobody wants to eat them."

Meanwhile Cindy has been to Mom's house for the appraisal and the buyers' inspections. She sends us an email asking why the door to the linen closet doesn't open. Mom has no idea why that would be. Next time we're at the house I go inside after watering the ivy and try the door to the linen closet while Mom sweeps. The knob doesn't turn. I jiggle it every which way, but it only moves a couple of millimeters to each side. I notice screw heads in the plate of the doorknob. They really should be on the other side of the door, but now I have something to work with. I retrieve a Philips head screwdriver from Mom's toolbox in the garage and minutes later have the door popped open. The knob that faces the inside of the closet has a locking mechanism of the kind that would be on the inside of a bathroom door. It was in the locked position.

I shake my head. There's no conceivable reason for the lock. Mom must have replaced the original doorknob with the locking one at some point, probably because the locking one looked newer. And then somebody put it in the locked position and pushed it shut. Was it Mom protecting her linens from open house riffraff? More likely she did it absentmindedly as we were locking up the house to leave. She denies everything when I ask, but what other explanation is there?

Not long after, she does something suspiciously similar at my house. She'd gotten into the habit of taking her lunch into the bedroom and closing the door, to avoid the cat messing with her food while she's eating. On this day, she set her plate down on the desk in the bedroom and headed back into the kitchen to get a fork, flipping the locking mechanism on the door and pulling it shut behind her.

"I was trying to keep the cat out," she explains to me five hours later when I get home to find her locked out of her room.

The linen closet isn't the only door at Mom's house with a wacky handle. The door between the kitchen and the back patio is like something out of a fun house.

"Who installed these door handles?" I ask her.

"I don't remember. It must have been the guy who remodeled my kitchen."

"If you flip the lever to lock the top lock and pull it shut from the outside, there's no way to get back in. You'd have to have the key to the front door and go in that way."

Mom shrugs. She's never had a problem with the way the doors lock.

On Mom's thirty-ninth day at my house, we hear from Cindy that the buyer's condo went into escrow and Mom can move back into her house to finish packing. We caravan to San Jose the next day, a Friday, to get a head start on the first weekend back.

We have less time than I thought. The contract had said thirty days from the time the buyer's condo goes into escrow to Mom's closing, but the date of October 4 that Cindy gives us makes it twenty-three days. Maybe the inspections and appraisals and contingency removals are all happening very efficiently. Neither Andy nor Mom remarks on it, so I don't either. We still have three full weekends to get everything done. We can do it. I think.

PART III

The Home Stretch

TWENTY-SIX

Back in the Saddle

September 14-20, 2019

It's our first weekend back at Mom's house. We're both quieter than usual. I'm not sure what's on her mind, but I can't stop thinking about these being our final weeks in the house. I've learned a lot in the last few months, and I'm hoping the remaining time with Mom will help it sink in. In the meantime, there's work to do.

We set things up in a few areas, being careful not to disturb the stager's furniture or props; she's coming for them on Monday. I make a little office for Mom by setting up her computer and printer on an end table and bringing in the rolling office chair from the garage. I reconnect the router and hook up the phone and internet, which takes a couple of hours, since I hadn't labelled all the wires when I disconnected them. We make a dining area out of folding chairs and a rickety TV tray. I pull the stager's bedspread and pillows off the daybed so

Mom can sleep in it, and I wrestle the futon couch out of the master closet for me. There's no spare pillow to be found, so I lay my head on my folded-up jeans to sleep.

On Saturday we make a trip to the credit union and the grocery store; this eats up half the day. The plan for the rest of the weekend is to pack most of Mom's remaining clothes and start on the kitchen. We have plenty of room to navigate, despite the stager's furniture. Even the front door opens all the way without hitting stacks of boxes and packing material. It feels weird not to work in a sea of clutter.

I suggest to Mom we get rid of the extra hangers, thinking this will be a short task.

"Why should I get rid of my hangers?"

"You have more hangers than clothes."

"No, I don't."

"All your clothes are on hangers, right? And here are all the extra hangers."

"Oh."

Now it turns into a project. She doesn't want to get rid of any plastic hangers, so she takes clothes off the cheap wire hangers and rehangs them on the plastic ones so that we only get rid of the wire ones.

After Mom heads to bed, I stand at the kitchen counter with my computer for another hour putting together slides for a presentation. I'm behind at work, and I'll sleep better knowing I don't need to do it tomorrow.

On Sunday I take everything out of the pantry while Mom finishes up with the clothes. It's not too bad—interspersed with the food items are empty boxes and about a dozen glass jars I set aside to recycle. Mom takes a look at the pile when she comes in.

She pulls out three of the empty jars that held a German brand of jam; she wants to keep them because "they look nice." She opens a plain glass jar that contains ground coffee and pours it into one of the jam jars, then hands me the empty jar. "Here, you can recycle that."

She retrieves the empty protein bar boxes from the recycle pile. "These are not ready to be recycled—there's one box missing that's not empty yet."

"You don't have to wait for the third box to recycle them."

"No. They go together. It's more efficient that way."

"But you'd have more room."

"I have enough room." She finds the third box, empties the remaining protein bars into a plastic cup, then reassembles the empty boxes into their original multipack. Now they're ready to recycle.

We work our way through several kitchen cabinets filled with gadgetry, most of which I've never seen in Mom's kitchen: baking tins, sifters, thermoses, tools for measuring and crimping and cutting, various types of racks and serving dishes. I keep reminding her of the small kitchen she'll have at her new place and that she won't have to cook anymore, and she gives up the majority. But these decisions are draining.

"I don't know if I can do this anymore," she says. "I feel like I'm getting rid of too much stuff just to get it over with."

"We're making good progress," I tell her. "Just a few more things and we'll stop for today."

I let her keep the two coffee grinders to make her feel better—they're small and she remembers using them for different things. The two crockpots are huge, however. They're barely used and have been stored in their original packaging. Mom takes the instructions out of the Hamilton box and tries to figure out if they go in the Rival box; then she matches up the names and returns the instructions to where she found them. She lets me take both.

I look around for something easier. The stacks of washed paper and plastic cups stashed behind Mom's dishes—I've had my eye on those for a while. I pull them all out. She lets me recycle eight of the ten stacks, promising she'll let go of one more on her last day in the house when she's sure she won't need them anymore.

The weekend wouldn't be complete without a rant by Mom about how put-out she feels by the process. Andy happened to mention that the couple who are purchasing the buyer's condo are motivated to get things done quickly because they're expecting a child.

"And I have to pay for it by getting out of my house sooner. Is it my fault they're pregnant?"

Good grief. I can't answer that logically without taking us down a rabbit hole. I go with diversion. "How would you like things to be?"

She thinks for a moment, then nods. "I would like to have all the time I need to sort through my things, without being pushed around."

All the time I need. Holy cow. Logic resurfaces. "You're not being pushed around. This is a transaction with multiple parties needing to move at the same time and everybody needs to make their plans. You're just first in line to move."

Mom juts out her chin. "But why is it only me that gets pushed around?"

I expect to have a quieter week since Mom is no longer at my house, but there's a constant stream of things that need my attention.

On Monday evening Cindy texts me to ask if the buyers can come look at the property on Friday around noon. I text Mom with the question. She doesn't respond, so I call her on Tuesday morning. Mom is okay with it and will probably skip lunch at the senior center to stay home and meet them. She's curious about the plans they have for the house. Mom sounds a little perturbed; I sense it's about Cindy going through me instead of contacting her directly.

On Wednesday morning Cindy texts me again to ask if Mom would be available to do the signing on Friday afternoon. I text back that I'll ask, but instead I agonize about it for a few hours. I text Cindy back and ask if she can send the information in a group email, since Mom is becoming a little sensitive about not being included. I'll follow up to make sure Mom sees it. Cindy apologizes and says something about not having access to her email because of computer issues. She asks me for Mom's phone number because that information is trapped in her computer.

Later on Wednesday, I call Sondra from Evergreen Meadows, Mom's first choice senior living community in Laguna Beach. Sondra and I have been emailing back and forth to address my miscellaneous questions, but she's stopped responding. I leave her a message to see if we can set up a time to talk on the phone and wait in vain to hear something back.

On Wednesday night I talk to Mom on the phone.

"Did my next mortgage statement come to your house?" she asks. Mom had her mail forwarded while she was living here, and we decided not to change it back, given she'd soon be at a new address.

"No, I haven't seen anything," I tell her.

"Then I'll have to go to the credit union in the morning."

"Why is that?"

"To get the loan number."

"For your mortgage? Why would the credit union have that? You don't have your loan with them."

"But they have my cancelled checks."

Eventually I figure out she's been communicating with the title company. They need her loan number, but she doesn't have anything with the loan number on it because she left her file boxes of current bills and important documents at my house.

"Why don't I take a picture of your latest mortgage statement with my cell phone and email it to you?"

"That sounds like a great idea. Now I won't have to go to the credit union."

Next, I bring up the signing. "Did Cindy talk to you about signing the papers on Friday afternoon?"

"No," Mom says. "It's the title company making the arrangements. They want me to be in Santa Cruz at 2 p.m." Then the battery on her phone gives out and we're done for the night. Cindy hadn't said anything about Santa Cruz—that seems rather far. I take another Friday afternoon off work so I can be there.

On Thursday I call Sondra again. There's still no answer, so I call the general number and ask if Sondra is available. She's not, but one of the move-in coordinators informs me that a one-bedroom unit recently became available. I gather all the information and leave Mom a voicemail, followed by a text. I have a lot to do at work and can't follow up with Mom until evening, then I repeat it all to her one more time.

"It's one of the larger one-bedroom units, on the fourth floor overlooking the trees on the back of the property. We can make a deposit to reserve it, then take a week or so to fill out the application and send it by email. We have until October 3 to show up in person so you can sign the lease and drop off a check for the first month's rent. Then you can move in."

The timing couldn't be more perfect. Mom's target date to be out of the house is September 29, but we'll have an extra day or two if we need it. I'm aware of how much I want Mom to get this unit so she won't have to stay at my house for an indeterminate amount of time waiting for the next one.

"That sounds good to me," Mom says. "Can we reserve it? I'll pay you back if you put the deposit on your credit card."

"Yes, I can do that. I'll call them in the morning."

Mom breathes a sigh of relief. "Now I know where I'm going to be living."

"Yes," I agree. "One more thing taken care of."

Then I ask about tomorrow. "So, Cindy and the buyers are coming to the house at noon, is that right?"

"Yes, they're coming at noon." Then, indignant, "Do you know what Cindy said to me?"

"No, what?"

"She said not to be dirty when the buyers come over. What did she mean by calling my house dirty?"

"I don't know what Cindy would mean by that—the house is not dirty."

Just as suddenly, Mom changes the topic. "Cindy wants me to go somewhere in the afternoon. She said something about signing off. Signing off for what?"

"All the paperwork to complete the process of selling your house."

"I don't remember doing anything like that before." She pauses. "But I'll do what she tells me to do."

"Would you like me to come and be there when you do the signing?"

"Oh," she snaps, "so they'll think I don't have a brain in my head, that I can't do anything for myself."

Geez, what brought that on? I take a breath and lean against the wall. "If you don't want me there, I don't have to go. I was just offering."

She turns immediately conciliatory. "Of course I would love to have you there. Even if you don't say anything, I'll feel more comfortable with you there."

"Okay, good. I'll bring my overnight stuff, and we can get an early start on the weekend again."

"You always think of the perfect ideas," she says.

We get off the phone. I've accomplished what I wanted but am exhausted.

On Friday morning I don't get anything done at work. I'm late because I had to pack my overnight things and empty the car from last weekend. Then I spend hours playing phone tag with somebody at Evergreen Meadows to take my credit card number and confirm the spot for Mom. By the time it's done, I'm a wreck and I can't concentrate. Good thing I took the afternoon off.

TWENTY-SEVEN

The Signing

September 20-21, 2019

It's the middle of the day on Friday, and I'm headed to Mom's house. Cindy and the buyers should already be there, but I'm not in a rush. It's okay if I don't meet the buyers—I just don't want to miss the signing of the papers at 2 p.m. The title company where the signing will take place is not in Santa Cruz, but in Campbell, just 15 minutes down the road from Mom's.

The Indian couple and their little boy are leaving Mom's house as I pull up shortly after 1 p.m. After they drive away, I knock on the front door and let myself in. Cindy is sitting on one of the folding chairs and talking to Mom, who is leaning casually against the wall. It seems the visit went well.

Cindy turns to me. "I'm sorry about all the texts this week. I was just telling your mom about my computer problems. My hard drive crashed, and I sent it to L.A. to get refurbished. Then when I got it back it was dead. I'm still waiting for a new one."

I give a sympathetic groan and roll my eyes. "What a hassle."

"I took my computer to get it repaired and they told me I had to get Windows 10," Mom says.

We collectively grouse about the Windows 10 operating system for a minute. Then the topic turns to timing. I tell Cindy we're having the pod delivered to the house next Friday, and we'll spend the weekend loading it with the remainder of Mom's things. It's scheduled for pick-up on Tuesday, October 1. We'll be out of the house by then, if not sooner. This is three days before close of escrow instead of five, but nobody remarks on it.

"What about the final cleaning?" I ask. "Does it need to be as thorough as the one that was done before we put the house on the market?"

Cindy glances at Mom and says in a joking way, "Your Mom thought I told her she was dirty. That's not it at all. I said it would be nice to have the house cleaned before the buyers move in. A lighter cleaning is fine."

"Sounds good," I say. "We'll do a lighter cleaning." This means wiping surfaces and the insides of cabinets, cleaning the bathrooms and the kitchen sink, and sweeping and mopping. We can do those things ourselves and not have to worry about scheduling someone to come.

Mom has been listening and smiling and not talking much. Now she walks over to the kitchen and microwaves herself a burrito for a late lunch. She excuses herself and disappears with it into the small bedroom.

Cindy looks at me and asks quietly," Is she all right? With everything?"

I have a fleeting thought that Mom got under Cindy's skin. I feel an urge to explain that Mom is *different*, to reassure Cindy she's not imagining things, but I chicken out. "Oh, yeah," I nod reassuringly. "She's fine." Then I prattle on about all the things I find unsettling and haphazard about the real estate process, as if this would account for any unusual behavior from Mom.

After Mom emerges from the bedroom, we all take a walk around the house. Cindy points to the wasp nest hanging high in the eave above the front door; the buyers would really like it taken care of. I add it to my list.

As we get ready to leave for the title company, I remember something from my document signing a couple of years ago.

"You should take your credit union statement," I tell Mom.

"Why do I need that?"

"They're going to want the information on the account where you want the proceeds to go."

"Oh." She finds the statement on the coffee table among the current papers and puts it in the folder with the other papers she's taking.

Janet at Summit Title has a firm and friendly manner. She adjusts to Mom right away, speaking more slowly and grasping her hand on occasion to get her attention. I'm surprised Mom doesn't object to being touched. A few years ago, I went with her to a doctor's appointment where she flinched and became testy when the nurse took hold of her arm for a blood pressure reading when she wasn't expecting it. But with Janet, Mom is a lamb.

Everything goes well until we get to the credit union statement. It doesn't have the routing number on it, and we'll need to call the credit union to get it.

"I can call them," I say, and I take out my phone. I've been making so many phone calls on Mom's behalf that I'm on autopilot. I enter the phone number from the statement and listen for the dial tone.

"I'll do the talking," Mom says.

Remembering her comment about being brainless and helpless, I tell her okay and put my phone on speaker. The automated system comes on and asks for her account number. I enter it from the statement, then I put the phone down on the table in front of her.

The lady at the credit union answers with a standard greeting. Mom says, "We are here at Summit to sign the papers, and they're asking for the account, and I don't see the information anywhere on here."

It takes self-control for me not to jump in and fill in the details Mom left out. I tell myself the credit union lady is a professional and she can ask for the necessary clarification. She does, and Janet interjects with a few of just the right words: Mom is at the title company signing escrow papers and we need a routing number to wire the funds. Everything gets taken care of.

Mom's eyes are glazing over. She can't

remember her social security number when it's needed on another form ten minutes later. She turns to me. "Do you know my social security number?"

"Um. I don't think so." I start looking through my notebook where I've been keeping track of all the downsizing and real estate details. "But you know it, right?" She thinks for a moment, then recites it. In the meantime, Janet has found it elsewhere in the documents and confirms it's correct.

During the remainder of the signing, Mom tries to make some of her usual quips and jokes, but it takes too long to set things up and get to the punchline. Her mask is slipping. *C'mon, Mom. Almost there.*

Finally, we're done. Cindy leaves in her car, and I take Mom home where she takes a long nap before dinner. She's not much use for the rest of the night, so I busy myself with a couple of the boxes of papers.

We have a few errands to do on Saturday morning. I volunteer to drive us in Mom's car. This usually involves listening to her detailed directions when we're going someplace that's on one of her familiar routes. "Get in the middle lane to turn left at the light, then get into the second lane from the right. The next turn is to the right but not until the third light, and most of the cars in the right lane will turn into the shopping center. So, wait to get in the right lane until after the second light." This drives Andy and Mike crazy; they both say something along the lines of, "Just tell me to turn left here and then right at the third light—I know how to drive."

Something feels out of whack when I climb into her car. The front seat is positioned close to the steering wheel and sits so high I need to scrunch down to see properly. Of course—Mom's hunched back. But then I notice the mirrors. Regardless of my posture, I have to crane my neck to one side or the other to see what's going on behind me.

"Your mirrors seem off. Can you see out of them?"

"Oh, I need to fix that. Mike put them that way for driving the last time he was here."

Yikes. That was what, nine months ago? I sit with my hands on the steering wheel and try to focus on this new puzzle. I don't want to mess with the seat since I don't want Mom to have to readjust it later. I don't want to mess with the mirrors in case I make them worse for her, and I don't want to have to remember to adjust them for her later. I decide not to adjust anything and determine to drive extra carefully. We head out.

Our first stop is the post office. Mom wants to fill out the change-of-address form for her new residence in person rather than online because she has some questions about when things will take effect. The young clerk isn't sure and recommends we ask at a different post office. Mom rephrases her questions a couple of times, and the clerk gives the same answer. By the time Mom asks for the addresses of the alternate post offices, I'm embarrassed and impatient. When we get back in the car, I punch USPS into my phone's GPS. There are locations that are closer than the ones the clerk gave us, and I tell Mom we're going to one of those instead. This turns out to be a mistake. I end up driving back and forth across an empty parking lot behind a mall, bent over in Mom's stupid clown car, trying to follow the GPS signal and peering at the back doors for a sign of an entrance.

I pull to a stop to gather my wits. Mom is neither critical nor supportive. She has an expectant look on her face that seems to say, "What are we doing next?" After apologizing for leading us nowhere, I ask Mom for the addresses from the clerk. We head for the one that's ten minutes away, which turns out to be inside a Hallmark-like store in a strip mall. The clerk there gives us more informed answers. Mom fills out the change-of-address form and turns it in.

Our next stop is a vacuum cleaner and sewing machine repair store. Mom wants to sell her old Singer sewing machine from Germany—it was still operational the last time she used it decades ago. The older dark-skinned gentleman behind the counter waves at the back room where we see rows upon rows of old sewing machines.

"You see all those? I don't need any more. I'll take yours, but I can't pay you anything."

"What about five dollars?" Mom asks.

He shakes his head. I hurry to get the sewing machine and paraphernalia out of the car and leave them on the counter before he changes his mind.

We spend the rest of the morning and early afternoon filling out the lease agreement and don't eat lunch until almost two. Then Mom takes another long nap before we turn our attention back to the kitchen. But we can't seem to get anything done. There are hordes of washed disposable containers Mom has collected and never used because she keeps reusing the same ones. This is an easy call, and she agrees, but we can't put them in the recycling bin until we've found the matching lids. There are drinking glasses I need a decision on, and I reach across her to point them out. She doesn't seem to see them, so I point again. She stares into the distance and starts to hyperventilate, taking rapid heaving breaths that don't subside until I back away.

Maybe tomorrow will be better. Leah's coming to help.

TWENTY-EIGHT

The Strawberry-Washing Bowls

September 22-26, 2019

It's Sunday, September 22. We have today and the following weekend to get everything out of the house, with another day or two of cushion if we need it.

Leah has offered to come and help pack, even though she has homework for her online graduate class. Before she arrives, Mom says, "I know she doesn't like me. She's probably just coming because of you, to help you out."

"Oh, I don't know about that," I say, flattered by the thought and thinking she's probably right.

We continue to work on the kitchen. I empty a drawer and prompt Mom to go through what I've laid out. It's an excruciatingly slow process. Mom wants to explain all her choices and see what I think. If my answer's not to her liking, she adds more explanation.

When Leah gets here, I direct her to the piles on the left of the kitchen floor. "These things need to be packed—Oma has already gone through them. Here are some boxes and packing material."

Leah surveys the piles. "Wait—which of this stuff is Oma is taking with her?"

"All of it. She's already looked through it."

Leah shoots me daggers with her eyes, but she sits down on the floor and starts packing. It doesn't take long before she confronts Mom. "You're moving into a one-bedroom place, and you'll be getting three prepared meals a day. Why do you need three full sets of dishes, a dozen vases, all this candle stuff, and all these little glass knickknacks?"

Mom sounds a little huffy as she replies. "This is my chance to have nice things. I'll finally have time to see what I have and use them because I won't be so busy cooking food all the time."

"But why do you need all these plastic cups? And all these bowls? You won't have room for them."

Mom walks over to Leah and squats down on her haunches to look her in the eye. "I've already looked at these things and I want them all. Plastic cups are useful to me in my daily life. And I need these bowls to wash strawberries."

"Three bowls? You don't need three bowls to wash strawberries." Leah points to another set of bowls. "And these?"

"Yes, I want those. They're important to me."

"But you're moving into a one-bedroom place. You won't have room for all this stuff. What are you willing to give up in order to keep those bowls?"

Mom points to the box that Leah just packed

with her day-to-day Corelle dishes, bowls, and cups.

"You're willing to give up your daily dishes that you use every day for this set of bowls that you never use?" Leah raises her eyebrows.

"Yes." Mom picks up the set of three strawberry-washing bowls and bangs them down on the floor one by one to punctuate each point: "I use *this* one to put them in, *this* one to drain them, and *this* one to clean them."

Mom stands up and turns to me, eyes flashing, and says bitterly, "I can't have anything nice. I have to throw everything away. I can't keep anything sentimental."

"No," I say quietly. "I don't think that's what she's saying."

"Oh, my ears must be fooling me. Or maybe it's my mind." She pauses. "I'm going to leave you two and go in the other room. I'm getting upset and I don't want to say something I'll regret." She disappears into the back of the house.

I take a breath. Leah and I exchange glances and get back to work.

I understand and agree with all the things Leah said. Mom is being unreasonable in the amount of stuff she wants to take with her. No question. And how do you deal with an unreasonable person? You are firm and direct and put your foot down. That's what Andy would have done. Mike, too. I'm the odd one out, the one who accommodates and engages with the unreasonable person to the point of exhaustion. I was an only child for seven years before Andy came along. That's a long time to be the sole focus of Mom's parenting efforts. I spent my energy figuring out how not to set her off. Challenging her on purpose was not in my repertoire; I'd tried it only once in my life, on the Thanksgiving after Dad died.

I'm glad Leah doesn't take after me. It's better to know how to speak up. Maybe some of the comments she made to Mom about her stuff will sink in.

Strangely enough, I also feel sorry for Mom. She was backed into a corner and saying ridiculous things to justify her choices. But I'm impressed she admitted her frustration and left the room to cool off.

When Mom comes out a bit later, she's in a calmer state. She tells me she'll have a protein shake for lunch. This means she's not expecting me to eat with her, and I'm free to have lunch with Leah. I can't wait to get out of the house—it feels like a pressure cooker. It occurs to me Mom might feel the same way and wants the house to herself for a while. Leah and I decide on a place, and we head out in her car.

Leah talks first. "I feel like it's such a waste of time packing all that stuff she doesn't need."

"I totally understand. I'm doing my best to talk her out of keeping things, and we've actually gotten rid of a lot. But at some point, it's not worth the energy to argue."

"Yeah, I know. But it's stressing me out—spending all this time packing useless things when I really should be home doing my homework. I wouldn't even be here if it weren't for you and wanting to help you out."

I smile. Then I'm struck by a pang of conscience. Mom made attempts to spend one-on-one time with my kids when they were young, because that's what her friends were doing with their grandkids. But my kids didn't relate to her, and I didn't force the relationships. When Leah was twelve, Mom invited her to a grandparents/grandkids weekend at Claire Tappaan Lodge with the Sierra Club. Leah didn't want to go, and I sympathized. I told Mom *I* was uncomfortable with the idea, and she dropped it.

I ask Leah, "What kinds of things did I say about Oma while you were growing up?"

"Nothing bad. It was a chore to spend time with her, and you acknowledged that. You said things like, 'Oh, that's just how she is.'"

"'A chore,' like how?"

"She'd talk about the minutiae of her daily life or whatever she was interested in. Like her visits with people I didn't know, or how she'd go to the grocery store and read the food labels. Super boring stuff. We never really connected on anything."

"Hmm."

"You and Uncle Mike talked about her being difficult in other ways, but I didn't understand what you meant until I went on that trip with her to Bangladesh."

"Ah, yes." Leah had called me and talked my ear off for an hour the moment she returned home. She was weak from food poisoning and jet lag, but she had to unload about Mom's crazy behavior.

When Leah was little, she thought of a grandma as someone to bake cookies with. On one of our trips to Germany, when Leah was seven, she remembers picking up Oma Martha's flour sifter. Opa Herbert scolded her, but Oma Martha said, "Lass sie doch" ("Let her be"). It seems both Leah and I prefer Oma Martha's company to Mom's. For the second time today, I feel sorry for Mom.

They manage to stay out of each other's way for the rest of the afternoon. Leah packs everything in Mom's pile, and Mom gives up an extra metal bowl and another two vases.

When Leah gets ready to leave, Mom says, "Thank you for coming over to help. I really appreciate it."

"You're welcome. See you next week."

"Oh," Mom says, pleasantly surprised. "See you next week."

The following week isn't nearly as crazy as the preceding one. By Thursday Mom has figured out she'll be in Southern California on October 4 getting settled into her new place, but that's also the day escrow closes on her house. She sends me a text.

"Do I need to be in San Jose on October 4? Have you talked to Cindy about that?"

"I think the paper signing last Friday was the last official thing where you had to be there."

"I have to be in Southern California to sign the lease or I lose the place. What if I need to be in San Jose? I can't be in two places at once."

"No. The signing was the last thing. We just need to let Cindy know when you're out of the house."

She sends me a third text. "Please read your answers to my questions. What has changed from the first to the second statement? Are you upset that I'm asking?"

What? I sigh and call her number. It goes to voice mail, but I don't leave a message. As soon as I hang up, Cindy calls me. She wants to know when we'll be out so she can schedule the final walk-through with the buyers. Also, we should be on the lookout for an addendum Mom needs to DocuSign. Before I get off the phone with Cindy, I confirm Mom doesn't need to physically be in the area for anything else.

I decide to text Mom back instead of calling. "I talked to Cindy," I start, camouflaging the fact that Cindy called me. "She said you do not need to be there at close of escrow."

Mom sends me emoticons: a heart and a smiley face. She thanks me for checking, and says she feels better. Good. So do I.

I send her a text to remind her that some of my kids are coming on Saturday to help, and I'm taking the day off tomorrow to come over and organize the boxes so they'll be ready to load into the pod.

She doesn't answer, so I add, "It's okay if you were planning to have lunch at the senior center. I can let myself in."

She sends me a text back: "You read my mind."

TWENTY-NINE

Dad's Last Wishes

1992

After Dad's funeral in early November, I went through his papers to take care of his final affairs. Dad had made a handwritten will in 1989 declaring his intention to leave everything to his three children. He specified a couple of bank accounts, his profit sharing proceeds, his pick-up truck, and a life insurance policy he'd had taken out in the '70s. When, as the executor of his estate, I called the life insurance company to collect on the policy, I found out Mom was still listed as the sole beneficiary and would therefore be the payee regardless of any other factors. Wills, handwritten or not, don't supersede the beneficiaries listed on a life insurance policy.

I sent Mom a copy of the policy, along with a copy of Dad's will.

"So, legally, it's mine," Mom verified over the phone after receiving the copies.

"Yes," I said, then waited for her to address the issue of Dad's wishes. Instead, she changed the subject. I was stunned but continued robot-like through the rest of the conversation.

After I got off the phone, I worked myself into a lather.

"How can she ignore Dad's will like that?" I asked Andy over the phone. It wasn't a huge amount of money when split three ways, and none of us was in desperate need of it, but it was the principle of the thing. "If she wants to keep it, fine. But she should acknowledge Dad's last wishes and tell us why she's not going to honor them."

"She should have said something about it," Andy agreed.

"We could bring it up next week at Thanksgiving when we're all together. What do you think?"

"Sounds good. We can talk everything out."

I called Mike about it, too. He was in his first year away at college and would turn out to be most in need of money, but he was noncommittal: "You guys go ahead."

At Mom's on Thanksgiving, with the side dishes warming and the turkey finishing in the oven, I caught Andy's eye. He nodded and walked over to the kitchen where Mom was drying her hands on a towel.

"Mom, there's something we want to talk to you about."

She turned to him. "Oh?"

My heart was pounding. Time for me to step up. I unfolded my arms and looked her in the eye. "Mom, you're disregarding Dad's last wishes."

"What wishes?"

"In his handwritten will, where he said he wanted everything to go to the three of us."

"Yes, and you have everything. You went and took all his paperwork and account information. I didn't get to see anything."

"You're divorced. I'm the legal executor. I'm supposed to take care of all the paperwork."

"And so?"

"What about the life insurance policy?"

"What about it? I'm the beneficiary. Legally, the money is mine. You said so yourself."

"Dad meant for that money to go to us. He said so in his will. He just never updated the beneficiaries on the policy."

Mom looked at me, wide-eyed and incredulous. "You think I should just give it to you?"

"It's not about the money," Andy chimed in. "It's about respect for Dad's last wishes."

"What difference does it make what his last wishes were?" Mom said. "He isn't here anymore."

I sucked in my breath and couldn't talk for a moment.

Andy spoke up. "So, you're planning to keep it."

"Yes," Mom said decisively. "I have reasons you don't know about. And I don't want to share them."

"That's fine," I managed. "But it would be nice if you said something other than, 'legally, it's mine.'"

"Well, what is there to say?"

"Maybe an acknowledgement that Dad wanted something different. It seems like you don't care—you're just going to ignore what you read in his will and say nothing."

"I went to his funeral. I paid my respects." Mom slumped down on the ottoman. "I feel so attacked. Really. You want the money that badly, that you would gang up on your mother like this?"

"We told you it's not about the money," Andy said. "You know us. We've never been that way about money."

"It's about acknowledging Dad's last wishes," I reiterated.

Mom's voice trembled. "I didn't do anything wrong. I can't believe you're attacking me like this, over money." She looked over at Mike, who'd been silent this whole time. "At least one of my children loves me."

I backed off and slunk over to the couch. This sure didn't go the way I anticipated.

Mom got up to take the turkey out of the oven and then disappeared into her room. The rest of us looked at each other and began subdued conversations about other things. After a while, we took the remaining side dishes to the table and started carving the turkey. Mom came back out, looking pained and long-suffering, and we all sat down around the table, not saying a word. Mom folded her hands and said a prayer of thanksgiving.

Oh Heavenly Father,

Thank you for allowing us to come together to share this wonderful food, for watching over us every day, and for blessing us with nourishment, health, and a roof over our heads. We are so grateful for your gifts, and we pray for your continued love and protection.

And please help my children who have just lost their father and are in deep pain. Forgive them their horrible words and actions against their mother who has nothing but love for them. They're grieving and they don't know what they're doing.

In Jesus's name,
Amen.

Andy and I didn't stay long after the meal, leaving Mike to spend the remainder of the holiday weekend with Mom. Good thing he hadn't gotten involved.

I look back on that Thanksgiving and pick apart all the mistakes I made—different ways I could have said things, different approaches I might have taken. I certainly should have picked a different day. Mike says it wouldn't have mattered—there was no way to do it that would have led to a different result. The only alternative would have been to say nothing about it at all, but I was tired of never saying anything. And I wanted to stick up for Dad. Mom's disregard of Dad's final wishes was the first and last thing I felt strongly enough to confront her about.

Sometime after that day, Mom told us about Dad taking her money during their separation; she'd thought about the life insurance money as payback. That made sense to me. But she never came to understand our point about honoring Dad's wishes. Not when Andy and I sat down with her a couple weeks after Thanksgiving and repeated what we'd said while she wrote it down verbatim in a notebook to study later. Not in the following decades, when she'd bring it up to me every seven or eight years: "I still feel so hurt by the way you guys went after me for that money."

She brought it up a couple of months ago after we started downsizing. "I've been trying for a long time to forget about that Thanksgiving after your father's death. But the memory still comes up and I feel hurt all over again."

I was dismayed. I'd always tried to correct her, telling her it wasn't about the money, but the message had never sunk in. "I'm sorry about that," I offered instead.

"Why did you act that way?"

I thought for a moment. "The week before, when we talked on the phone about Dad's insurance policy, you were very businesslike about it. Abrupt, even. It upset me."

"So, it was the way I talked?"

"Yes."

"That could be," she said, nodding slowly. "Thank you. That's helpful."

She reached out her hand. "Friends?"

I took her hand and shook it. "Friends."

THIRTY
Helping Hands

September 27-28, 2019

On Friday morning I engage in a weekly ritual I look forward to abandoning: I unload all the stuff in my car from last weekend before I drive to Mom's. I throw out scratched up kitchen tools, plasticware, and cutting boards. I salvage six boxes of kitchen stuff. I'm keeping one, and the rest I put back in my car to drop off at Goodwill on the way.

In five days we'll be on our way to Southern California. I'll drive us in Mom's car with her vacation supplies and her most essential things. We'll stay the night at Andy's. The next day I'll take Mom to sign the lease at her new place. Andy will lend Mom an air mattress and a folding table and chairs to use in her unfurnished apartment until the pod arrives the following Tuesday. By that time everything will be in Andy's hands, since I booked a flight home on Saturday.

Andy calls me and puts me on speakerphone to

include Julie. "We noticed you're not staying the whole weekend like you usually do," he says. "What's the matter? Don't you like us anymore?" They laugh. They understand I'm exhausted and need the extra day to myself.

Once I'm back home, my car will be waiting for me in my driveway. I can leave it full of junk after this weekend and drive it around that way for as long as I like.

When I get to Mom's house, the pod is in the driveway. I don't need to open it until the kids get here to help tomorrow morning. There are other things to take care of in the meantime. I call Mom's utility companies to have services cancelled a week from now, on the official closing date of escrow. I try to set her up with internet service at her new place, but I run into issues—the automated system isn't picking up the numbers I tap on my phone, and there's no way to connect with a live person. I switch to my computer and spend an hour online with Katy, the chatbot, picking out the right package deal for Mom, then I leave it in the cart without finalizing the set-up when it asks for the last four digits of her social security number. That's all I need right now, to argue with Mom about why they would need that information when I'm questioning that myself. I can't deal with it anymore. While Mom is in the bedroom sorting through clothes, I sneak into the pantry with my water glass and pour myself a shot of bourbon from one of Mom's bottles of liquor.

Mom knows about the real estate document she's supposed to sign, but cheerily announces she doesn't have to use DocuSign—Cindy left a message on her answering machine that gave her other options. "Oh, really," I say. After dinner we listen to Cindy's message which says no such thing. Mom's face falls. "Well," she says, "I'm not doing it tonight." Then she goes into a rant about being a cog in a machine and everything having to be done through the computer, all so the software companies can get their profit at the cost of people who might not even have a computer. Aren't they human, too? What if *she* didn't have a computer?

While Mom putters around to get ready for bed, I go into the garage to get the boxes organized for the kids to load into the pod tomorrow. I come back into the house to ask Mom something and she says, "Can we shut that door so the mosquitoes don't get into the house?" I don't see any mosquitoes. But I start shutting the door to the garage whenever I come through, even though it might be only ten seconds before I go back through again. I pour another shot of bourbon and sneak it into the garage with me.

The next morning Leah shows up at ten with my son Nick and his wife Magen. Magen takes one look at me and says, "Oh, I'm so sorry," and comes in to give me a hug. Apparently, I look as tweaked and haggard as I feel. And it's not from the alcohol.

I put them to work dismantling the remaining pieces of furniture. I unlock and open the panel door of the pod and am greeted by a jumble of boxes. Andy had tied the lighter stuff down with ropes, but not well enough to keep it in place on the way to and from Milpitas for storage. I reorganize a bit before the kids take over. Soon most of the furniture and packed boxes are in the pod. Mom no longer has access to her daybed, but she can sleep on the futon couch which will go on the pod last. I'll make do with blankets on the floor.

The kids order pizza and beer and go to pick it up. I join them for lunch in the park next to Mom's house, since Mom wants to eat her microwavable lunch burrito and not have to worry about anyone else.

After lunch I have them to go through a dozen boxes of old newspapers, magazines, bills, and junk mail. This time I won't take the excess home in my car. I made an appointment with Junk King to come Monday afternoon and clear out whatever's left.

As the kids get ready to leave, they ask Mom about her new place and tell her they're looking forward to seeing it.

"Oh, you'll come and visit?" Mom says. Then she turns to Leah. "But you won't, will you?"

"What?" Leah frowns in confusion.

Mom tilts her head a little and smiles. "I asked Leah once if she would come to visit me after she goes away to college, and she said, 'No,'" emphasizing the word with a head nod.

Leah stares at Mom. "I never said anything like that."

"Oh yes you did." Mom nods slowly with knowing eyes.

"I'm not having this conversation," Leah says and walks out the door, leaving Nick and Magen staring wide-eyed.

"That's okay," Mom calls after her. "We don't

have to talk about it again."

Nick and Magen regain their composure. They say their goodbyes and hurry outside to catch up with Leah.

An hour later I get a call from Leah. Her computer is here at Mom's. She had taken it to do homework in case we needed them to stay late, and then she forgot about it.

"Say no more," I tell her. This is an excuse for me to drive home for the night. Which makes me inexplicably happy. It means an extra hour and a half on the road before I'm back at Mom's in the morning, and I'll be spending most of the time away sleeping. But I'll wake up in the morning and get to be alone with my thoughts for a while. That sounds good to me. Really good.

THIRTY-ONE
The Final Days

September 29-30, 2019

On Sunday morning I'm on my way to Mom's again. I soak up the view along Highway 84. It's the beginning of fall—the rolling hills are still straw colored and contrast nicely with the speckling of dark green trees and shrubs. I'll make this trip at least once more; I took the afternoon off work tomorrow so I can be there when the junk removal people come. If we can get everything else done by then, that'll be it.

We're down to three categories: things that go in the pod, things that go in Mom's car, and things that go in the pile for junk removal. In the first category are about two dozen boxes of papers we didn't get around to sorting and the remaining household items that still need to be packed. But before I work on those, I have a couple of pesky tasks to cross off my list.

The Terminix guy came earlier in the week to take care of the wasp nest in the eave above the front door. He knocked on the door and told Mom to stay inside while he was working, but she couldn't tell if anything was different after he left. When I came on Friday, I found sizable chunks of the nest still hanging from the eave. Smaller pieces of nest and dead wasps were sprinkled on the walkway beneath and on the nearby bushes. I went online to give Terminix a bad review. I decided I would try to remove the remainder myself but hadn't gotten to it yesterday.

 I get out Mom's tallest ladder. She insists on helping me carry it from the garage around to the front door and then holds it while I climb up. I'm armed with a long stick I use to poke at the nest remnants which are still a good four feet above my head, gently at first to make sure nothing comes after me, then harder to dislodge them. The pieces stick to the eave tenaciously. I manage to scrape off about half before I quit in frustration. Not a productive start to the day. I use the stick to take down the yellowjacket trap hanging next to the remnants before I climb down—who knows how long that's been there. I find a couple of plastic bags and put one inside the other to collect the wasp-related debris for disposal. I nearly jump out of my skin when I notice some of the wasps in the clusters moving. But they are sluggish, in their death throes from the pesticide. After I get it all into the doubled-up bag, I tie the top and toss it into the trash. At least I didn't get stung.

 My other task is to take down the hanging lamp in the kitchen that Mom wants to take with her; she had it spelled out in the real estate contract. It's a pretty lamp with a nice brown, beige, and off-white pattern but otherwise it's nothing special. I look up at it and regret I didn't try to talk her out of it. A couple of hours and two trips to Home Depot later, the lamp is in a box and the disconnected wires are properly insulated and hidden behind a ceiling cover plate.

Now it's 2 p.m. Mom ate one of her convenience meals during my second trip to Home Depot. I haven't had lunch, but I don't feel like taking a break. I start working on several boxes in the garage that are falling apart, transferring the papers into new boxes while pulling out old magazines and newspapers for recycling. Mom walks up to me and asks what she should work on.

"You can take everything out of the bathrooms."

She disappears for a short while, then comes back into the garage and asks me again.

"Have you taken everything out of the bathrooms?"

"Yes."

"Why don't you go through the food in the kitchen and pantry and separate out what you don't need in the next week? We can pack that up to go in the pod."

Mom agrees and goes back inside. I follow shortly after to take a peek at the bathrooms and confirm my suspicions—there's still stuff on the counters, under one of the sinks, and hanging on the doors. Never mind. We'll get it all done eventually.

I go back to the garage and continue working. It's not long before Mom calls me inside to look at a couple dozen items segregated on opposite sides of the pantry. She points to the ones on the right and begins reciting her thoughts.

"These sardines would be nice to eat with salad when there's no other meat. These canned soups and beans will keep for a long time. These bottles of liquor don't have very much in them."

I interrupt her. "Do you have a question? I'm trying to focus on the stuff in the garage."

"Oh, yes," says Mom. "Do these things go in the pod?"

"Yes," I say, irritated once again at having to answer such questions. I find her a couple of large plastic totes. "All those kinds of things can go in here."

Sometime later she comes out to the garage again.

"Do you know where my chamomile tea is? I can't find it."

"I packed all the teas already. Do you want me to look for it in the packed things?"

"No, no—I have some tea." She disappears into the house and comes back shortly with a reusable Trader Joe's shopping bag full of teas and nuts. "I had this in the small bedroom. See, there's green tea, mint, and lemon. And there—chamomile. These would be great to have in the pod. But if we do that, I would want the nuts taken out."

I stare blankly at the bag.

"Confused?" she says.

"Yes. You're telling me a lot of things, but I don't know what you want me to do. Do you want those in the pod?"

"Yes, but not the nuts."

Stay calm. We're so close to the end. "Can you take the things out that you don't want in the pod?"

She takes out the nuts. I remind her to take out the chamomile tea, too.

By 5 p.m., most things are packed, and I start loading boxes into the pod. I don't have a strategy for arranging and securing everything, so there's a lot of trial and error. As daylight fades, I abandon my goal of fitting the mismatched boxes together perfectly and start stacking them in uneven piles—I need to know if everything will fit in the pod before I go home today. I can rearrange and tie things down properly when I come back tomorrow; the pod won't be picked up until the following morning.

I fix us the usual salad, protein, and crackers for dinner, making note of what's left to eat tomorrow. I leave for home after 8 pm. There's still a fair amount to do, but I'm feeling pretty good. We're going to get it done. Just one more day.

On Monday I leave work at noon and head for Mom's. I'm bringing my lunch and also a couple of hard-boiled eggs from home to supplement the food she has left—it's a good bet we'll still be here at dinner time. Once the pod is ready and the junk gets taken away, we still have to pack Mom's car and do a light cleaning. Mom is happy about the eggs and wants to save them for dinner, but the protein shake she had for lunch wasn't enough. I offer to split my Gouda cheese sandwich with her. That hits the spot.

While Mom naps, I consolidate the piles for junk removal on one side of the garage. It's mostly old dusty cardboard boxes and papers to be recycled, crumbling particle board shelving, warped or cracked plastic household things, and a few items to be donated. The latter include Mom's bicycle and the Formica kitchen table and chairs I grew up with.

Next, I tackle the large cardboard boxes perched in the rafters of the garage. I know they're empty because I lifted the corners months ago when I was taking stock of everything in the garage. Mom saved the original boxes for various household appliances and gadgets so if these items ever needed to leave her house they could do so in their original packaging. One large box is for a giant TV that predated flatscreens and that she got rid of years ago; there are smaller boxes nested inside. At this point, she can't argue that she still needs any of them, since all her appliances and gadgets have been packed in other boxes. I look inside each one to make sure they're empty and add them to the junk pile.

The satellite dish antenna in the rafters has me worried, but I find it surprisingly light and have no trouble getting it down. That goes in the junk pile as well.

Now I'm ready for Junk King, and it's almost four o'clock. I'm glad they didn't show up right at the start of the three to five o'clock appointment window. While I wait for them to arrive, I open the pod and mentally toy with how to rearrange and tie down the things I loaded yesterday. I move a few things around, but I don't want to get too engrossed in case they show up. I spend an hour in this unfocused state, becoming increasingly worried as five o'clock rolls around. What if they don't show? At 5:11 I get a call saying they'll be here in twenty-five to thirty minutes. I'm immensely relieved.

A covered dump truck pulls up with a crew of three. The guy in charge eyeballs the stuff covering one-third of the garage floor and gives us an estimate. I learn that the estimate is based on volume, and I haven't flattened any of the boxes. Mom's next-door neighbor, who's been offering to help if we need anything, has come outside to see what's going on and sees his opportunity. He takes all the empty boxes that are still in decent shape to his house. He'll break them down and put them in his recycling bin until they're gone. This reduces Mom's total by $50, down to $268. Mom agrees to the price, and they get going.

I stand back and watch as the crew goes back and forth, and the last remnants of clutter slowly disappear. More and more solid ground comes into view. I feel a rising sense of elation—the burden is lightening right before my eyes.

After they leave, I focus my full attention on the pod. The odd-shaped items are a headache, particularly Mom's living room armchairs which don't stack and have angled surfaces and curved arms into which nothing fits. I wedge them on top and try to figure out how to tie them to keep them there. Then Mom comes out. In my earlier unfocused state, I had offered to drive to the nearby Sprouts to get her a ready-made salad after I finish loading the pod. Now she asks about dinner, which is the last thing on my mind. I stand there numbly, unable to make a decision.

"But you really want to finish loading the pod, right?" she offers.

"Yes," I say. "I really don't want to stop for anything until the pod is ready to go."

She goes back inside, and I return to what I was doing . . . which was becoming frustrated because I'm not remembering how to do things. I've forgotten how the ratchet mechanism on the tie down strap works. I can't replicate the knots that I knew how to tie yesterday, and I mess up a perfectly good knot that I spend half an hour trying to re-tie.

Mom comes back out almost an hour later. I can feel her looking at me, but I ignore her.

"So, you're not going to Sprouts," she says.

I explode inside. *Clearly I'm not done loading the pod. Don't you see how hard I'm working? Can't you ever give me a break? Why don't you take care of the food and bring me something to eat?* But that's not fair, is it? I had told her I would go and that's what she has in her head. Out loud I say, "I don't know. I'm just having a lot of trouble with these knots."

"That's okay. I can take care of myself. I know where to get things to eat in my own house."

There's no rancor in her voice. It almost sounds like she's trying to reassure me. Now I feel guilty on top of being irritated and frazzled. She goes back inside, presumably to eat her hard-boiled eggs along with whatever else she can scrounge up in her own house.

Half an hour later she brings out a couple of hanging jewelry organizers with plastic pouches.

"Where can I hang these?"

I'm not sure what she means and am too distracted to ask. I point to the shelves on one side of the garage.

She walks over and hooks the hangers over the edge of one of the shelves. "We can't forget about those."

"Uh-huh," I nod.

She comes out a bit later when almost everything is in the pod and I'm a bit calmer. I point to the jewelry organizers and say, "What did you want to do with those?"

"Can you hang them somewhere in the pod?"

What? "No, we shouldn't just hang them in the pod."

"Oh, you can lay them down. I took all the jewelry out." She goes back in the house and comes back with a handkerchief full of jewelry she hands to me. "Those I don't want." Then she shows me a small pouch. "These I want to keep. Can we put them with any of my other jewelry?"

"You mean the jewelry we've already packed? I'm not sure I can find that box in the pod."

"That's all right. Why don't I just put them in this briefcase?"

I don't argue. While she's doing that, I get some bags to contain the hanging organizers, which still have jewelry in them. I tape the bags shut.

Finally, after a second hour in the pod, I'm done. I lock it up and have a final planning discussion with Mom. We still need to pack her car and clean, but we'll do that tomorrow. Mom can spend one final night in her house. The futon couch is in the pod, so Mom will sleep on a pile of blankets. I'm going home and coming back in the morning. We'll finish by lunch and then caravan to my house where she can spend the afternoon relaxing while I go to work. We'll spend Tuesday night at my house before heading to Southern California on Wednesday.

I feel giddy hearing myself describe it. I'll be flying high on the drive home.

Then Mom says, "And what will we do for lunch?"

THIRTY-TWO
Just a Couple of Hours Cleaning

9 a.m., October 1, 2019

When I get in the car on Tuesday morning, food is the last thing on my mind. I'm usually fine without breakfast, but once I'm on the road to Mom's, my stomach growls. I rummage around in my purse with my free hand and find an old, squished protein bar.

I'm not surprised to see the pod still in Mom's driveway when I arrive; the confirmation message we received last night specified a pick-up window from 10 a.m. to 1 p.m. But I am surprised when I walk through the front door and find a few items of clothing hung inside the hall closet. It was empty when I left yesterday.

Mom sees me looking. "Those I want to hang on the inside of the car," she says.

Three small suitcases sit near the front door. They are next to a pile of odds and ends that will go in her car: the TV monitor, her computer, and a plastic tub of pantry items. Good. Mom got her clothes all packed.

I spy something in the pile that gives me pause: a fancy cookie tin I'm sure I threw in the trash yesterday, contents and all. Inside was a mishmash of items that looked like they were from a memory game: a bottle of nail polish that had leaked and glued itself to the tin, a record player needle, a bobbin of thread, a bottle of Wite-Out, a wooden chicken head that had been part of a toy, a small dropper bottle of odor eliminator, and an unidentified electronic part.

"I thought I threw this away," I say, pointing at the tin. "Did you go through the trash?"

"Yes," she says. "I want to keep that. I like it."

Let it go, I tell myself. We have bigger fish to fry. Then I survey the rest of the house and my heart sinks.

Most everything is still spread out all over the place, some of it more so than when I left last night.

There isn't much left in the kitchen, but what's there is spread over as much counter space as possible. Mom's washed breakfast dishes, a box of crackers, a small packet of lemon juice, a lid from a plastic container to hold used tea bags, the cap to a pen, the plastic mats that protect the counter from wet dishes, plastic containers containing miscellaneous plastic items, a couple of boxes of tea, a folded dish towel, a book of Bible verses, a planner notebook, the plastic tray of apples, a small container of plum tomatoes, a phone handset, a Brita pitcher, washed plastic lettuce containers, plastic bags, and still usable pieces of paper towel. There's a dish towel draped over one of the cabinet doors under the sink, on top of which lay two old disposable gloves, discolored from use.

The doorknob of the linen closet, once again and for what will be the last time, has clothes hanging from it.

I peek in the laundry room that I know was empty yesterday. A couple of damp washcloths and a small towel are draped across the closed washing machine.

"I used those this morning," Mom says. "They aren't dry. Where am I supposed to put them? Or am I not allowed to clean myself?"

I wonder why she would go into a different room to hang them instead of in the bathroom where she just used them, but I hold my tongue. I've got to conserve my energy. "We should gather everything that's going in your car in the same place, so we can see how much there is. And we'll be less likely to forget something." I take the damp things out of the laundry room, drape them across some small empty plastic bins, and put them next to the other things in the living room.

I take a quick tour of the bathrooms. "There's still stuff in there," I tell her.

"What?"

"The bathrooms. There are still things in the bathrooms. Towels and toiletries, and some things under the sink in the master bathroom."

"Oh, I thought I got everything out." She goes into the master bathroom and comes back with the items from under the sink to show me. "You were right, there were still things in there."

In the small bedroom, her sleeping pad, blankets, and pillow are laying out. There are clothes hanging in the closet, and more suitcases and sturdy plastic shopping bags scattered around on the floor. She's not done packing her clothes.

I close my eyes and take a deep breath. I don't know why I expected anything different. When I recount this to Andy and Julie in a few days, Andy will call me silly for expecting Mom to actually be packed and ready to load her stuff into the car, and Julie will groan with her head in her hands that it reminds her of their kids.

I resign myself to the fact that we won't be done by lunchtime. I decide it's a good time to wipe down the insides and outsides of the kitchen cabinets with Murphy's Wood Oil. This will be a calming activity that will keep me out of Mom's hair while she continues her packing process.

Five minutes after I start on the cabinets, she walks up to me. "Is it okay if I take a break? I want to run a few errands and say goodbye to the neighbor in the corner house before I get too tired."

I tell her yes. After she leaves, I put down my rag. This is a good time to clean the bathrooms—she won't be here to complain that they weren't clean enough for me, or to keep me from tearing out the icky shelf liners because they're still good and the new owners could use them. I'm doing the sinks when I hear the sound of back-up warning beeps. After I finish the bathrooms, I go outside and look. The pod is gone.

I'm nearly done with the kitchen cabinets when Mom comes back. It's close to lunchtime and she needs to eat. She microwaves herself a breakfast burrito from the freezer, then goes to lie down for her usual twenty minutes after eating.

I disassemble the internet and phone, then sweep the floor of the garage and swipe away all the spider webs. Mom had some concrete cleaner we left out to clean the garage floor, but I've changed my mind about doing that.

When Mom gets up, I tell her I want to start packing the car and ask if everything that will go in it is assembled in one place.

"Oh. I should pull my car into the driveway, now that the pod is gone. With the back to the house so it's easier to pack."

"Yes, that would be good."

I go outside a few minutes after she does, to put some cleaning supplies back in my car. Her car is in the middle of the cul-de-sac, facing away from the house. Mom isn't used to backing in. Her car jerks backwards in stops and starts as she looks back and forth between the on-screen rearview guide and her mirrors. I realize the garage door is closed and go inside to open it. I hesitate for a moment because I don't want to startle her or confuse her backing up process, but then I go ahead. She's already turned the car off and started climbing out, but she gets back in when she sees the garage door opening. She continues backing up the car, starting and stopping and turning the steering wheel back and forth. It's exhausting to watch, but somehow I can't look away.

Once the car is fully in the garage, she turns it off and gets out. "Should we close the garage?"

"No," I say a little too sharply, not wanting anything to do at the moment with mechanical moving things. I start loading the car. It takes a while to finish, but it's a methodical and almost soothing task.

"What do I do now?" she says after I close the trunk.

"There's still stuff in the bathroom."

"No, everything is out."

"In the middle section, where the bathtub is."

We walk back there.

"Oh. You are right. I forgot that stuff." She grabs the shampoo, bodywash, and towels.

I pick up the conditioner.

"Oh, that's almost empty," she says. "You can leave that."

What? I ignore her and take it.

She shows me the doubled-up towel she was using as a floor mat and starts talking about it. "I would prefer to use this as a towel, but it's got this." She shows me a large rip in it. "I can still use it to cover things."

Why, oh, why are you bothering me with this? I nod and murmur assent. I can't afford to get her upset or drain what little stamina she has left. We have a drive through rush hour traffic ahead of us; soon the commute from San Jose to Livermore will increase from forty-five minutes to twice that or more.

We have only a few things left to do. She'll sweep the entire floor of the house, and I'll follow with a wet mop, using the leftover Murphy's Wood Oil to make the place smell nice. I give her a head start on the sweeping while I deal with the remaining food in the fridge. I bring in the cooler from my car and empty the fridge and freezer contents into it. The freezer has a built-in ice-cube maker that's covered with a row of hard plastic teeth. There's a bag of gel ice stuck in them. I don't know how to release the teeth. I spend twenty minutes wrestling with the gel pack, pushing and pulling and twisting to get it unhooked. My frustration builds until I feel like I'm in one of those dreams where a never-ending stream of obstacles keeps you from leaving the house. I rip the plastic and get sticky gel all over my hands, but I still can't get the bag out. We will never finish. I'm stuck here at Mom's house forever. A few strangled curse words escape my lips. I get an old pair of scissors from my car that Mom didn't want, and I hack through the rest of the plastic. It finally unravels, but leaves slippery ice gel all over my hands and inside the mechanism, with no obvious way to remove it for cleaning.

Mom comes over. "Is everything all right?"

"There was a bag of ice gel stuck in the ice cube maker. Did you know about that?"

"Yes. They said they couldn't do anything to fix it."

"Who?"

"The refrigerator repair people. Did you fix it?"

"I got the bag out, but there is gel all over. If I had more time to work on it, I might have figured out a better way."

"Maybe I should have traded in this refrigerator

to get one that works better."

"There's nothing wrong with the fridge—it just had the gel bag stuck in it."

I wipe off as much gel as I can from the freezer and wash my hands several times. I leave a note for the new owners: don't use the ice in the ice cube maker—there is ice gel inside. I need to wipe down the inside of the fridge, but I can't find any cleaning supplies—not even a sponge. They must have gotten packed in Mom's car. I grab the Pine Sol from my car and use paper towels—that'll have to do.

Mom has finished sweeping the bedrooms and hallway and continues with the rest of the floor as I start mopping. We work together quietly for the next ten minutes, after which I've caught up with her and we have only the dining area left. Now she's tired and has to lie down. I finish sweeping and mopping and dump the water out front.

Finally, at four o'clock, everything is out, and the place is clean. We take some final pictures, then strategize how to close up. We need to pull the car out and close the garage from the inside, leave the garage door opener and house keys in the kitchen drawer, then pull the front door shut with the latch in the locking position.

"Are you ready?" I ask. "I'm pulling the door shut now and we won't be able to get back in."

"Well, why would I want to go back in?" Aside from the puzzled look on her face, I see no trace of emotion. I guess she's already said goodbye to the house.

Well, good. The better to pay attention to the road on the way to my house. That will be the last hard thing.

THIRTY-THREE

Sunset

4 p.m., October 1, 2019

Mom follows me on the freeway as we head to my house. I glance in the rearview mirror often to keep an eye on her; it's probably been a while since she's driven in traffic this heavy.

Mom rides my bumper—she doesn't want to lose sight of me. This reminds of the time we caravanned on a camping trip, and she pulled in right behind us at the gas station even though she didn't need gas, blocking others in line who did. Other than the tailgating, she drifts a little to the left or to the right, but always within the lines. I minimize lane changes and slow down when someone gets between us, so they'll go around.

In the meantime, I try to figure out my emotions. I should feel relieved to be done with the house and apprehensive about Mom driving in rush hour traffic, but I just feel numb. This matches my reflection in the rearview mirror.

DOWNSIZING MOM

At long last we exit the freeway at Highway 84, which is also backed up. There's a section after the transition where two lanes merge into one, but Mom is determined to stay right behind me and doesn't follow the zipper rule. As we crawl along, the other driver has plenty of time to dwell on the fact that Mom is not letting him in. I sneak glances at him in my mirror and over my shoulder, ducking my head a little so he won't know I'm associated with her, and implore him by telepathy: please don't mind her, she's just a little old lady.

Eight miles and thirty minutes later we've broken through the traffic and are waiting at the light to turn left onto my street. It's less than a mile to my house. I take a deep breath in through my nose and blow it out slowly through pursed lips, relaxing my shoulders. Not much can happen now.

The light turns green and I go. After I make the turn, the sun glares at me, low and bright. I pull my visor down and feel a flash of irritation at how long everything took today and that we had to drive home so late in the day. It takes a few seconds to shake my pique and get back to my Zen state. Then I glance in my rearview mirror and panic.

Mom is not right on my tail. She made the turn, but her car is at least a football field away and receding. Something's wrong. I slow down, but she's not catching up. She's completely stopped in the middle of the road. What could be the matter? A couple of cars go around her. I pull over to let them pass and look back over my shoulder.

Now Mom's car is moving, but slowly. Should I turn around and drive back? What if she's having a stroke and about to run into another car? Or God forbid, a pedestrian? Maybe I should get out of the car and run back on foot.

Now she's going a little faster. Maybe it's a problem with the car. That would be bad news since we need to drive it four hundred miles tomorrow. She gets closer, and I pull into the street to lead us home. I look back again. She's drifting to her right, directly toward a parked car. Holy crap! Maybe I was right about the stroke. Then she stops and backs up towards the curb. The car comes to rest at an angle with the front a little into the street. Oh, thank God.

I pull all the way over, grateful that I didn't hit any parked cars myself. I turn off my car, pull out the key, and run back to Mom's car. When I get to the driver's side, I'm short of breath and apprehensive. She has her hands on the steering wheel and is looking straight ahead, but she seems okay. She sees me and opens the car door.

"Are you okay?" I ask.

"I can't see," she says, and again I think stroke. "I've never seen the sun glare through the car window like that."

My first reaction is relief. She's all right. My second reaction is disbelief. All that back and forth, all that stopping and starting, all that erratic driving, and that's all it was—a dirty windshield? Then irritation. Irritation that she couldn't have dealt with it in a more straightforward manner that didn't scare me half to death. But I have my calm face on.

"Do you want me to drive your car to my place? We're not that far away. I can walk back to pick up my car."

She agrees and goes around to the passenger side. I get into the driver's seat and see, against the setting sun, the filmiest car window I've ever encountered. I suppose I can't blame her for not noticing—she probably hasn't driven the car at this time of day for a long time. "We should clean the inside of the windshield before we leave for Andy's tomorrow," I say. "It looks like it has a lot of buildup on it."

I maneuver the car the remaining half a mile home. I know the curve of the street and where the other streets connect, so I know where to watch for other cars; most of my attention is devoted to scanning for pedestrians. Of course, this would be more difficult for someone who is less familiar with the route, even more so if they need extra time to process sensory information and unfamiliar situations. My final feeling about this episode is gratitude that Mom erred on the side of safety—she didn't do anything reckless to keep from looking stupid. Which is anything *but* stupid.

I back Mom's car into my driveway.

"Where did we put the car cover?" she asks.

"It's in the pod."

"Well, that wasn't a good idea. I could have used it to cover the car, so people wouldn't see there's stuff inside."

"It should be fine," I tell her, since there's nothing we can really do about it. "My neighborhood is safe and quiet."

I go to open the front door for her so she can go in and relax, but she stops me.

"Are you going back to get your car?"

"Yes."

"Can I come with you? I could use a walk."

We head out on the sidewalk. It's getting cold and I'm only in my red tank. I didn't think to grab a jacket because I've been so focused on getting us to my house and settled in, which has been mind-bogglingly elusive. Ten minutes later we reach my car. My heart catches in my throat as I see the half-open car window with my purse on the passenger seat. I had been so frazzled about Mom's potential stroke that I had forgotten to secure my car. But my neighborhood is safe and quiet, and everything is intact. I'll take it as a happy ending to a long day and a good omen for the trip ahead.

We drive back to my house, and I park out front. I take the cooler of food inside, then go back for the cleaning products so they won't bake in the heat during the day. Everything else I leave in the car: assorted cleaning implements and hand tools, kitchen and household items that Mom decided at the last minute she didn't want, a final batch of cardboard boxes, bags, and plastic containers for recycling. My poor car. It will need a thorough vacuuming when it's empty again someday.

I make us Gouda cheese and egg sandwiches with roasted cauliflower for dinner. Mom expresses her appreciation and goes to bed.

Now, finally, I get to relax. After five months of hard work helping Mom downsize, sell her house, and find a new place to live, all the pieces are falling into place. Mom will be set in her new retirement community, and Andy will be nearby looking out for her. All that's left for me to do is take her on one final road trip. The eight-to-ten-hour ride in Mom's car, taking her to sign the lease, getting her settled in—piece of cake. I can handle anything that comes up. I feel invincible, and I will sleep well tonight.

Job well done.

As for the other goal I had in helping Mom downsize, about revisiting the past and our relationship and getting to know her as a person, I feel like I hit the jackpot. I'm still processing everything I've learned, but one thing is clear: my feelings about Mom have changed.

Throughout my childhood and much of my adulthood, I saw her as a powerful, imposing figure who purposefully manipulated us with guilt and her irrational temper. I marveled at the way she could talk circles around me—nothing I said made a difference other than making her angrier or giving her more ammunition. Being able to label Mom's behaviors helped me see them as patterns associated with specific conditions, and not to take them so personally. And I did always take them too personally.

When I was young, I absorbed the message that there was something shameful about my core self, and that it was better to stay invisible. Out in the world, I looked at the ground to avoid eye contact and rounded my shoulders to make myself look smaller. I didn't want to attract the attention of the exuberant types who might think I was too quiet and put me on the spot. Straightforward logical conversation was manageable, usually, but the language of feelings and human interaction made me either bumbling or mute. Which sounds . . . autistic.

A bit of internet research points to something else: social anxiety. While both autism and social anxiety can result in awkwardness and reduced eye contact, the underlying reasons are different.[43] In autism, the roots are neurodevelopmental: a difference in wiring makes it hard to absorb the social rules and rhythms that come intuitively to neurotypical people. This wasn't me. I could follow the flow of a conversation without conscious effort. I was aware of tone, volume, and taking turns, and I understood sarcasm, reading between the lines, and inferring intent. My problem was when the attention turned to me and I was expected to speak. This often triggered a fear-based physical response in line with anxiety: racing heart, blank mind, shortness of breath, breaking out in a sweat. Such reactions lessened over the decades, but I never outgrew them completely. Getting an education helped. It gave me confidence there were parts of the world I could master without having to understand people and their complexities. After that, Corporate America forced me to build my communication skills and taught me other things, such as how to accept positive feedback with grace rather than suspicion.

I had a distorted view of emotions in my early

---

[43] Olivia Guy-Evans, "Differences between Social Anxiety and Autism," Simply Psychology, updated December 6, 2023. simplypsychology.org/social-anxiety-vs-autism.html.

years. Feelings were bad. They clouded the picture and made everything worse. They were how you hurt other people. I ignored my feelings and instincts because they weren't helpful—they gave me no useful information I could act on. Instead, I clung to logic, but it was no match for Mom's convictions. She was so insistent on her way of seeing things, including what *my* feelings, thoughts, and motives were, that I always wondered if it were true. I ended up questioning my perceptions, intuition, cognitive abilities, and my decency as a human being. If this was love, I wanted no part of it. Feelings could go jump off a cliff, too. I was well into adulthood before I realized how important emotions were in figuring out what made people tick and where the problems were.

I still have residual ways of seeing the world that come from my upbringing. I expect to be misunderstood, and to have my opinions disregarded. I shrink from people's strong emotions and am uncomfortable around authority figures. I avoid conflict and I wrestle with self-doubt. God forbid I impose on anyone or say the wrong thing and bring scorn on myself. In most facets of life, I'd rather blend into the background and be invisible. In the end, though, I learned to get along in the world in my own quiet way. I have patience, adaptability, and humility. My habit of hanging back and observing, and continuously questioning my own conclusions, makes me a more careful and thorough scientist. I can piece together practical ways forward when things get complicated. In an ironic twist, waiting to speak until I'm sure of what I'm talking about makes me come across as wiser.

I also have traits that I share with Mom. I'm absent-minded and I obsess about things. I have my own problems with organization, and I hang on to too much stuff. I say awkward things and don't always hew to social convention. It used to irritate me when people pointed out the similarities between us, and I would actively try to act in the opposite way. But it doesn't bother me anymore.

Mom had her own challenges. Underneath the chaos was a human being who wanted the same things as me: to feel accepted and supported by the people around her—to have an influence on them, to matter to them. This seems ludicrously obvious, but it's the first time I've *felt* it.

Another new sentiment I'm feeling is admiration for Mom—not for her achievements, but for her personal qualities. When I was young and could see almost nothing else, I noticed her persistence and resourcefulness, her desire to learn about and get involved in the world, her work ethic, and her ability to charm people. ("Don't worry," she'd say as she waded into questionable waters, "I'll be nice to them.") Those qualities didn't matter much to me at the time, but now I can appreciate them. And maybe add a few more to the list: courage, optimism, and a certain compassion for those who are marginalized by the system.

The experience of autism has been described as living in a foreign land where you don't have a full grasp of the language.[44] Mom was always searching for a place where she felt at home. San Jose might have come the closest. She made a life for herself there. She had a career, a house she bought and maintained, friends, church, and social activities. She was part of the community. Now she'll have to start over somewhere new. I hope it doesn't take her long to make new friends who appreciate her as interesting and worthwhile.

I give a final glance at the clutter lining the walls of my house before I go to bed. I'll need to do my own downsizing when I get back from Southern California. But it's not a problem—I'll take care of it when I get back. Or later. Everything is all right now.

---

[44] strangerdarkerbetter, "A Stranger in a Foreign Land: Understanding the Autistic Experience," So Much Stranger, So Much Darker, So Much Madder, So Much Better, May 31, 2018. strangerdarkerbetter.wordpress.com/2018/05/31/a-stranger-in-a-foreign-land-under standing -the-autistic-experience/.

EPILOGUE

It's October 2020. I'm in the card aisle of the Rite Aid drugstore in Livermore, searching for the right card for Mom's birthday. I never felt much inclination to send cards on birthdays and special occasions. How meaningful is it to sign your name below someone else's words and stick it in the mail? I guess it's in the eye of the beholder. When we were downsizing Mom's belongings in 2019, she refused to throw out a birthday card she had received from her insurance agent in 1997. "That's the only birthday card I got that year," she'd said.

A year has passed since we moved Mom into her accommodations at Evergreen Meadows, the senior living community in Southern California. After the move, I established a routine of calling her once a week, figuring the predictability of talking to someone familiar would help her settle in. This was not a trivial decision. Before the downsizing, I'd left it up to her to call me when she had something she wanted to talk about. If I started calling her every week, it would become a long-term commitment that would be hard to back out of. I berated myself for my childish resistance, but the truth was, after everything I had learned about Mom, it still took effort to communicate. It was *work* to manage our conversations and mitigate misunderstandings. I promised myself a glass of wine during our weekly call on Sundays at 3 p.m. if I felt I needed fortification. And this has been the case every Sunday since. Although sometimes it's beer.

After the first three months, Mike and I drove to Southern California to visit her and Andy's family for the holidays. Mom was still adjusting to the new routines and faces. "It doesn't feel like home yet," she told us. "I feel like I'm still on vacation." She did her laundry once a week in the laundry room a few doors down from her apartment. She attended fitness classes on Mondays, Wednesdays, and Fridays at 10 a.m. Every Sunday morning she went to the little onsite theatre to see a live stream of the sermon from nearby Saddleback Church. She went for walks and short drives in her car, and had found the local CVS, DMV, and branch of her bank. She was thrilled to no longer be dealing with all the food-related chores. She often found the daily specials unhealthy, but there were always alternate items from a standard menu. The staff soon learned her favorites: salmon, steamed broccoli, and a double portion of the green salad with no dressing. And always an extra apple or orange that she took with her and squirreled away in her room. There was a Trader Joe's she could walk to when she wanted to supplement the food she was getting with her favorite snacks: cucumbers, grapefruit, and avocadoes.

On one of the days of our trip, I arranged for Mike and me to join Mom in the dining room for lunch. I should have known better. Mom chattered on about the food choices: "You could get the broccoli instead of the carrots. Or you could get an extra side serving of broccoli and have it with the carrots." Mike frowned and said icily: "We've already ordered our food." Belatedly I remembered Mike's aggravation about eating with Mom: "I can't stand this infernal fussing about food," he'd said to me. Things took a while to thaw out after we went back to her room. Eventually they started talking about our family history in Europe, a topic of interest to them both, but by then it was time to leave.

Mom asked me if I would take a box of her things with me that she no longer needed. I peeked inside before putting it in my trunk. Among other things was the set of three strawberry-washing bowls she had fought with Leah to keep. Andy also gave me multipacks of Press'n Seal plastic wrap she had given him but that didn't fit in their drawers. How was it that I was *still* driving home with Mom's stuff?

During one of our calls in January, Mom asked, "Have you heard about that Coronavirus? Are you worried it might come here?"

"No," I said, "it sounds like it's just in Asia and that one case in Washington. I'm sure they're taking all the precautions to contain it."

It's not the first time in my life I've been wrong about something. A couple of months later the pandemic was spreading in the US, and California had instituted a shelter-in-place order. At Mom's complex, they closed the dining room and started delivering the meals to residents' rooms. Exercise classes and Bible study were cancelled until further notice. The residents were required to wear masks whenever they were outside their rooms. Luckily, Mom could still go outside for her daily walks. But she was not supposed to go inside the Trader Joe's, so Andy bought grapefruit and avocados and dropped them off for her at the front desk. Mom and Andy met clandestinely a few times while she was out walking, since visitors were not allowed inside, and she wasn't supposed to mingle with anyone outside.

In April she said, "You know, I'm so very glad to be here, and so grateful for everything you did to help me get here. Can you imagine me having to deal with this Coronavirus thing if I were still in my house in San Jose?"

Indeed. My relief at being done with the downsizing had increased manyfold with the onset of the pandemic. "I'm so glad you're doing well and that they're taking such good care of you," I told her.

A couple of months later, the restrictions were wearing on her. "This isn't how I imagined things would be," she said. She still made comments about what a relief it was she didn't have to prepare her meals, but now they alternated with complaints that she felt like she was in jail. Instead of getting to interact with people and visiting her grandkids, she felt isolated. "I look forward to your phone calls all week," she told me.

Early in the summer, some restrictions were lifted. The dining room reopened in shifts with socially distanced seating. Outdoor exercise classes and indoor Bible study resumed with social distancing. Plastic barriers were installed in the sitting area outside where residents could reserve a spot to see visitors in person. Andy and his family came to visit in July; Mom said it was very nice. A couple of months later, Mom got to see the family again when Andy picked her up to join them on a walk.

Mom started interacting more with the other residents, and I'd hear about the occasional interchange. "That guy across the hall wants something from me," she said in a coy voice. "He keeps inviting me to his room. I told him I'm not interested in a relationship. I don't need a guy telling me what to do—I already did that once." In September, she told me the lady who leads the Bible study didn't want to talk to her anymore. "Oh, well," she said. "That's how it goes. It's the same here as everywhere—some people like you and some people don't." She paused. "But most people here are really very nice."

I'm rooting for Mom to make new friends. It would be nice if she found someone autistic. I can think of one friend in Mom's past who might have been autistic; they were like peas in a pod when I saw them together. I used to consider Joyce an odd duck, but that description doesn't seem right anymore. She was a never-married sociology professor, friendly and direct and talkative, but not in an extreme or awkward way. She traveled alone and collected artifacts from all over the world. She had an extensive collection of Christmas decorations and turned the inside of her three-bedroom house into an elaborate display every year, complete with electric trains. I got to see it once and it was impressive. Joyce's house was full of stuff, but it wasn't out of control like Mom's had been. The most peculiar thing I ever saw Joyce do was spend most of the night grimacing and covering her ears against the loud music at Andy and Julie's wedding reception.

During Mom's downsizing, I found cards from Joyce in which she shared details of her day-to-day activities and the health issues of her aging cats. There were also photocopies of political cartoons she thought Mom would enjoy. In one card, she reminisced about a recent visit from Mom: "I had a wonderful time. I consider myself fortunate to have such a compatible friend. Now it's back to 'grubby reality.'" Mom's odds of finding another such compatible friend aren't great. According to the CDC, the prevalence of adults in the United States with ASD (autism spectrum disorder) is 2.2 percent; if we're talking just women, it's less than one percent.

Now it's October and things are looking up. There's promise of a vaccine and returning to some semblance of normalcy in 2021. Mike has his plane tickets to the Bay Area, and we're planning our usual road trip to Southern California if Covid case rates stay low. We'll see.

Mom's birthday is next week. I thought I would have an easier time finding a card for her, but I've already been in the Rite Aid for half an hour. These cards are awful—either too mushy or so bland that they don't say much at all. What an aggravating ritual.

DANIELA FRITTER

I find a card that talks about family and sharing a bond and that the recipient matters to the sender. It's close, even though it has a line in it about love and laughter that's not quite right.

That's the one. I sign it:

Love, Daniela

AFTERWORD

Readers who are interested in learning about less obvious presentations of autism may find the book *Is This Autism?* helpful.[45] The authors have combined their research, clinical experience, and life experience into detailed descriptions of what autistic traits can look like when the autistic person masks or when their personality is less oriented toward external expression. These descriptions are augmented with the subjective experiences of autistic people through quotes and vignettes. Despite the outward appearance of blending in, differences in physiology and internal perception and processing in these individuals can still lead to stress, exhaustion, and other health problems.

My mother's formal diagnoses include depression and generalized anxiety disorder, both conditions that commonly co-occur with autism, but not autism itself. She might also have hoarding disorder, based on the similarity of her behavior to that of Jessie Sholl's mother in the memoir *Dirty Secret*,[46] and the symptoms outlined by the Mayo Clinic.[47]

Although my mother's borderline personality

---

[45] Donna Henderson, Sarah Wayland, Jamell White, *Is This Autism? A Guide for Clinicians and Everyone Else* (Routledge, 2023).

[46] Jessie Sholl, *Dirty Secret: A Daughter Comes Clean About Her Mother's Compulsive Hoarding* (Gallery Books, 2011).

[47] The website for the Mayo Clinic; the "Hoarding disorder" page. mayoclinic.org/diseases-conditions/hoarding-disorder/symptoms-causes/syc-20356056#.

behaviors significantly influenced how I felt about her most of my life, the focus of *Downsizing Mom* is on autism, because this was the path to understanding her. Readers who are interested in BPD are encouraged to do further research.

Downsizing Mom is not intended to be a balanced portrayal of autistic and nonautistic points of view. It is written from the perspective of the nonautistic narrator who is just becoming aware of how differently her undiagnosed autistic mother has always experienced life.

ABOUT THE AUTHOR

Daniela Fritter is a career physical chemist who was drawn to creative non-fiction and narrative poetry later in life. She is a regular reader at the local open mic, and a couple of her poems have appeared in the Peregrine Literary Journal. *Downsizing Mom* is her first book.

Daniela writes about emotionally complex themes from her personal life, with a journalistic eye, relatable language, and a dose of humor where possible. Her analytical style blends physical details, multiple perspectives, and timing to tell engaging and holistic stories. Her favorite topics are relationships, personality typing, psychopathology, neurodiversity, and dementia.

Daniela was born in (West) Germany and immigrated to Southern California with her family when she was eight. Her English skills surpassed her German skills by the time she was a teenager.

Daniela lives and works in the San Francisco Bay Area. She enjoys reading, wine, travel, and spending time with her three grown children and their families. She is treasurer of the California Writers Club Tri-Valley Branch. Connect with her on *danielafritter.com*.

www.ingramcontent.com/pod-product-compliance
Lightning Source LLC
LaVergne TN
LVHW091625070526
838199LV00044B/942